D0391287

THE

PALMISTRY BIBLE

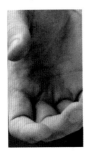

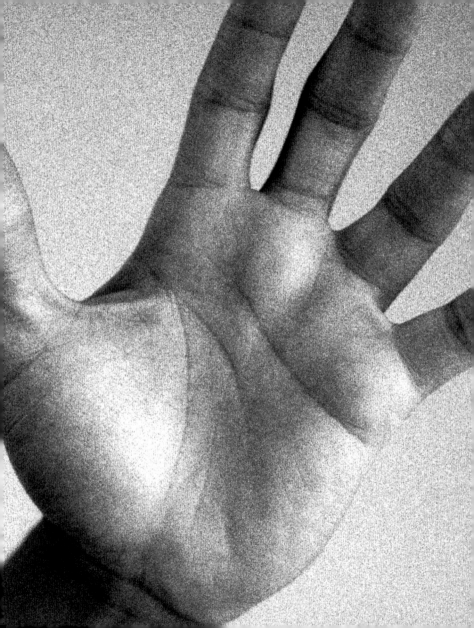

THE
PALMISTRY BIBLE

THE DEFINITIVE GUIDE TO HAND READING

Jane Struthers

STERLING

New York / London
www.sterlingpublishing.com

With love and thanks to everyone at
Fox and Howard, without whom . . .

Palmistry Bible

Library of Congress Cataloging in Publication Data Available

10

Published in the U.S. in 2005 by Sterling Publishing Co., Inc.
1166 Avenue of the Americas, New York, NY 10036
Distributed in Canada by Sterling Publishing
c/o Canadian Manda Group, 664 Annette Street,
Toronto, Ontario, Canada M6S 2C8

First published in Great Britain in 2005 by
Godsfield Press, a division of Octopus Publishing Group Ltd
Endeavour House, 189 Shaftesbury Avenue
London WC2H 8JY
www.octopusbooksusa.com

Copyright © Octopus Publishing Group Ltd 2005

All rights reserved.

For information about custom editions, special sales, premium
and corporate purchases, please contact Sterling Special Sales
Department at 800-805-5489 or specialsales@sterlingpub.com.

Printed in China

ISBN 978-1-4027-3007-8

CONTENTS

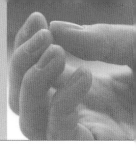

INTRODUCTION

If you want to learn about someone's character, look at his or her hands. Even if that person is a complete stranger and you only see him or her for a short while, the shape of the hands and fingers will tell you a lot.

The more you look at someone's hands, the more you will learn about that person. Every element, from the texture of the skin to the gaps between the fingers and the patterns made by the lines on the palms, tells its own story. When you learn to read hands, you are developing a fascinating new skill that you can practice everywhere, simply by observing the hands of the people around you.

This part of the book introduces you to palmistry, explaining exactly what it is and what it can tell you about other people. It also answers such points as whether the lines on your palm can change over time, and tells you how to give responsible palm readings.

THE HISTORY OF PALMISTRY

Where and when did palmistry originate? As with so many other divination techniques, it is difficult to say for certain, because its precise origins have become lost over the centuries. Even so, palmistry is thought to have started in the East more than 5,000 years ago. There are Indian, Chinese, Japanese and Korean writings on palmistry dating from this time, but it was centuries before this ancient knowledge of palmistry crossed over to the West.

A SECRET KNOWLEDGE

When palmistry finally arrived in Europe, probably in the early Middle Ages, it was largely undocumented and

Palmistry was was condemned by the Catholic Church during the Middle Ages.

spread by word of mouth. Before the advent of the printing press, writing materials were precious and few people could read, and the scribes who wrote out documents were usually

For centuries, palmistry was closely associated with gypsy fortune-telling.

busy with other tasks, such as government or religious treatises.

Besides, palmistry was thought to be nothing less than fortune-telling, and the Church had a great deal to say about such activities. Just as tarot and astrology were associated with Devil worship and other nefarious practices, so palmistry was actively discouraged. In an era when women could be burned at the stake on suspicion of being witches, no one wanted to make themselves the target of bigotry and intolerance by displaying seemingly diabolical gifts that enabled them to see into other people's hearts and minds. Palmistry was also widely connected with gypsies, who (like wise women) were persecuted throughout most of Europe. Nevertheless, a small number of books on palmistry were published in Europe from the 16th century onward, although they had a very select audience.

THE RISE OF PALMISTRY

Palmistry really began to become established in the 19th century, thanks to the upsurge of interest in all things occult. Spiritualism took the West by storm and palmistry became widespread. At long last popular books on the subject were being published, although some of these were inaccurate and sensationalist. Well-born women who spent their days enjoying genteel pursuits loved the idea of being able to read character and destiny in their own hands and in those of their friends.

PALMIST TO AN EMPRESS

At first palmistry was largely the province of women. One of the most

Napoleon Bonaparte's military and political careers were shown in his hand.

celebrated early palmists of the 19th century was the Frenchwoman Marie-Anne le Normand. She was a gifted tarot reader, but she invented most of her palmistry knowledge as she went along, always insisting that her predictions were correct. They were certainly very accurate when she read the palm of a young general called Napoleon Bonaparte, who had just married Marie-Anne's client, Josephine de Beauharnais. Le Normand prophesied a glittering military career that would make Bonaparte the most famous man in France. Her predictions came true, and Bonaparte set such store by le Normand's readings that he was appalled in 1809 when she predicted that he would divorce Josephine, who was by now his empress. He was so disturbed by these predictions (which described his secret plans in alarming detail) that he took the precaution of having le Normand imprisoned until the divorce was safely over. This was wonderful publicity for her, and she later wrote a book about her work with the Empress Josephine. Unfortunately it was full of bizarre palmistry "facts," which showed that she had only the vaguest grasp of the science, even though her predictions were correct.

Cheiro had a very high opinion of his skills, which his many clients shared.

CHEIRO

One of the most famous palmists of the early 20th century was Count Louis Hamon, who called himself Cheiro (from the Greek word for "hand"). He was a brilliant self-publicist with an overactive imagination about his own exploits and experiences, but he was also a highly skilled palmist whose clients included the most famous and respected people of their day. He wrote several books, some of which are still in print, and he is still the best-known palmist of his day.

WHAT PALMISTRY SAYS ABOUT PEOPLE

Your hands do not lie. You can disguise almost everything else about yourself, from the way you speak to the shape of your nose, the size of your stomach and the color of your hair, but you cannot change the size and shape of your hands. For a palmist this is a blessing, because it means that your personality, habits and instincts are written all over your hands, ready to be interpreted by anyone who has the necessary skills.

When you begin to practice palmistry, you will discover how useful these skills can be. Even if you do not want to devote your spare time to reading the palms of your friends and loved ones, you will learn a lot about them simply by looking at their hands. You will discover who is the bully and who is the victim, who is the shrinking violet and who is the life and soul of the party, merely by observing the shape and size of people's thumbs and fingers. You will learn a secret code.

Even the way someone holds a wine glass will tell you about his character.

A handshake can be very informative about someone's attitude to life.

This is invaluable information because you can use it to study the hands of other people whom you meet. If you are going for a job interview, take a discreet look at the hands of your prospective boss or colleagues when you first meet them. Do you think you will get along well with these people? Does the shape of the boss's hands complement the shape of yours, or is it so different that you are on totally different wavelengths?

Look at people's hands when you meet them in social situations. Would you like to get to know them better, or can you already see that for some reason you will not get along? Palmistry is also invaluable when you are talking to salespeople. Take a look at their hands as they give you their sales pitch to decide whether or not you should believe them. You will be amazed by what you see!

WHAT IS PALMISTRY?

Palmistry enables you to discover a person's character and the events of their life by interpreting the shape of their hands and the formation of the lines on their palms. It is remarkably accurate, and it can seem astonishing that so much information about us is stored in our hands, ready for other people to read. So is palmistry an art or a science? Perhaps it is a combination of both, because it combines the intuition and sensitivity that are so often part of an art with the knowledge and experience that are required to practice a science properly.

FORTUNE-TELLING
Palmistry is often dismissed as nothing more than fortune-telling, a phrase that conjures up images of crossing with silver the palm of a mysterious crone before she peers at your hand and announces that you are going on a long journey. But if you start to think about it, you might wonder what is so wrong with having your fortune told? Is it the notion that you are surrendering all your responsibilities and decisions while someone tells you what you are going to do with your life? Are you afraid to be told what might happen, in case it comes true—whether you like it or not? We will discuss the concept of free will versus fate a little later in this section (see page 20), but you might want to start thinking about it now.

THE SCIENTIFIC APPROACH
In our technological age many of us pride ourselves on being thoroughly rational, believing that nothing exists unless we can view it through the lens of a microscope, a telescope or some other scientific instrument. Equally, if we cannot explain why something

happens (for instance, why homeopathy works when the fewer active ingredients there are in a remedy, the greater its effectiveness), we may assume there is no merit in it and that we can therefore dismiss it as

Palmists often study a client's hand with the help of a magnifying glass.

a figment of our imagination, or as bogus. Some people like to apply this argument to palmistry and other divination techniques: They cannot explain them and therefore they do not work. But do we have to understand everything that happens, or dare we welcome a little trust and magic into our lives? You may not be able to explain how palmistry works, but that doesn't have to prevent you from using it and learning from it.

THE FOUR BRANCHES OF PALMISTRY

Originally palmistry was divided into two sections, known as chirognomy and chiromancy. Chirognomy is the art of reading character from the shape and size of the hand, fingers and thumbs, while chiromancy is the art of reading the lines on the hand. These two original branches of palmistry have now been joined by two contemporary

fields of study, known as body language and dermatoglyphics.

You may already be familiar with body language, in which psychologists draw conclusions about people's character and motives from the way they hold and use their bodies. It is

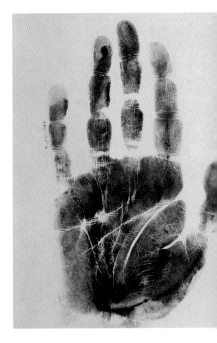

This hand print clearly reveals both the major and minor lines on the hand. Study of these lines is called chiromancy.

described in more detail later in this section (see pages 30–31), to help you use this technique in your own palmistry readings. Dermatoglyphics originated in the 1830s in the study of fingerprints and has progressed dramatically since then. Scientists have realized that not only our fingers, but our whole palms, are covered with minute skin patterns that are unique to each of us, and which can be analyzed to provide valuable information about our characters.

In palmistry, the relatively modern study of fingerprints and other skin markings is called dermatoglyphics.

SELF-KNOWLEDGE

Palmistry describes both your past and future, because all the major events that affect you will be shown in your hands. If you use palmistry only to find out about the past and the future, you are ignoring its very valuable ability to tell you all about yourself. Palmistry can describe the strengths and weaknesses of your character, which will help you to become more

aware of who you are and, as a result, to develop psychologically, spiritually, mentally and emotionally. You may also become more tolerant and forgiving of others once you are aware of your own shortcomings, because you will realize that these are a part of being human. That does not mean you can use them as excuses for bad behavior: blaming your arrogant

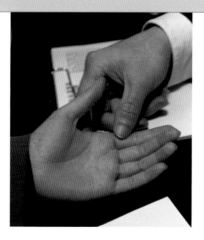

A good palmist will examine both hands, not just the dominant one.

tendencies on your long Jupiter fingers, for example, or your reluctance to stand up for yourself on your thin thumbs. However, you may become aware of your stumbling blocks, which could help you to navigate your way around them in the future.

After palmistry has outlined your strengths, you can start to play on them. For instance, if you are fed up with your current job and want to switch to something more interesting, or even retrain for a new career, your hand will give you plenty of guidelines concerning what might suit you. It will tell you whether you are highly imaginative or rooted in practicality, whether you thrive on a hectic schedule or need to take your time over things. These are all valuable pieces of information about yourself that you can use to your advantage.

WHAT PALMISTRY IS NOT

For centuries the Christian Church has disapproved of palmistry because it is regarded as a way of telling fortunes. Some people even believe that palmistry is linked to the Devil, or that terrible things will happen to them if they have their palms read. However, palmistry has absolutely no connection with Satanism or with unleashing malevolent forces that will wreak havoc in your life.

Palmistry is not a branch of astrology or the tarot, either, although these techniques are sometimes mistakenly grouped together. There are simple links between astrology and palmistry, because the hand shapes are named after the four astrological elements, and the mounts and fingers are named after the seven planets of traditional astrology, but that is where the connection ends. Palmistry and astrology are entirely separate disciplines, both of which have a great deal to teach us about ourselves.

Palmists used to be stereotyped as mysterious and rather weird women.

FATE VERSUS FREE WILL

Is your future already determined by fate, or can you change it? Was it fate that made you pick up this book? If you use it to predict what is going to happen to you in the future, are these predictions set in stone, even if you do not like them?

Each person's hand is unique, as you will discover once you start to read palms.

THE RELIGIOUS POSITION

The answers to these questions will vary according to your religious or spiritual beliefs. Some religions teach that everything you do throughout your life is preordained. It is as though you are responding to a set of preprogramed instructions, although of course you do not realize it at the time. Other beliefs teach that you are in control of your own destiny, which is always in a state of flux.

KARMA

Many people believe in karma, which is the doctrine that says that you reap what you sow. At its simplest level, if you eat too much chocolate, you will feel sick—this is a clear example of cause and effect. However, karma becomes much more complicated when you start to deal with larger issues, such as whether the circumstances of your present life are the direct karmic result of your actions last week, or even whether they result from a previous incarnation.

The answers—assuming that we can even attempt to find answers to such huge questions—are beyond the scope of this book, but they do have a bearing on palmistry because of the theory that your future is determined by your present. Does this mean that the lines on your hand describing your future will change if you start to behave differently, or is everything predestined anyway, so that you need not worry about such things? Although you may not have the answers, it is helpful to ponder these questions when you become interested in palmistry. If you do not ask them of yourself, someone else surely will.

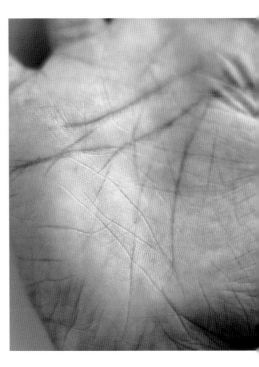

Do you have to accept the future that is shown by the lines in your hand, or can you alter your destiny?

DO THE LINES CHANGE OVER TIME?

Do the lines you were born with stay the same or change over time? Actually, the lines on your hand do change, sometimes in a surprisingly short time. This does not mean that your heavily afflicted heart line, complete with all those stress lines describing past broken relationships, will magically iron itself out when you meet Mr. or Ms. Right. The lines showing your past experiences will not change, but the lines describing your future may well do so. This can also happen if you become aware of a

A baby's hand contains all the lines you would expect to find on an adult's.

The lines on a hand will change subtly as the person's circumstances alter.

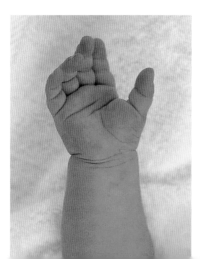

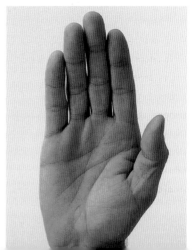

difficult situation that will end in disaster unless you correct it. If you take avoiding action, the lines describing the problems that lie ahead will start to alter so they eventually tell a different story.

PALM PRINTS

In order to discover this for yourself you need to become familiar with the lines on both hands. Study them carefully, and preferably record them by taking palm prints (see page 26) and dating them. You can then take further palm prints six months or a year later and see if there have been any changes. Look for subtle differences between the two sets of prints, especially in the areas of your hands that describe what has been happening to you lately. For instance, if you have recently changed jobs or discovered your vocation, check the areas of your hand (such as your fate line) that relate to your career.

Starting young

One of the best ways to discover how people's hands change over time is to record them right from the beginning of life. It is fascinating to chart the changes that take place in children's hands as they grow up, and the prints will give you a wonderful record of their life.

Sometimes you will find what seem to be inexplicable changes, because you cannot relate them to your current experiences. When this happens you can assume that your hands already know something that you do not. Take note of these changes and see what happens. You will be fascinated as your life begins to reflect the events and changes already shown in your hands.

RIGHT OR LEFT HAND?

Before you start a reading it is essential to ask the person in question whether he or she is right- or left-handed. The significance of the lines on the dominant, writing hand will be different from that of the lines on the nondominant hand.

SAME PERSON, DIFFERENT LINES

Take a close look at the palms of your own hands. How do they differ? Are some of the lines much clearer on your dominant hand than on your nondominant hand? At this stage you do not need to know what the lines actually mean, or even what they are called. Simply observe the differences between the lines on your two palms. Close observation is one of the keys to being a good palmist. Perhaps you have particular lines on one hand, but not on the other, or the same lines but in different formations? For instance, one of the major lines may end in different places on each hand, or might be much more strongly marked on one hand than on the other.

THE DOMINANT HAND

Your dominant hand is the one you write with. The lines and other markings on it describe the events that have taken place in your life and what you can reasonably expect to happen in the future (although you must always bear in mind that these lines can change). In other words, the dominant hand describes what is real in your life. It shows the skills and abilities that you are equipped with right now, and which you can draw on at any time.

THE NONDOMINANT HAND

This is the hand you do not write with. It describes your potential and what

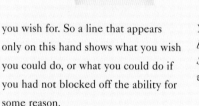

you wish for. So a line that appears only on this hand shows what you wish you could do, or what you could do if you had not blocked off the ability for some reason.

IF YOU ARE AMBIDEXTROUS

If you are adept with both hands, you probably still find it easier to use one hand rather than the other to write with, and for the purposes of palmistry you should consider this hand to be your dominant one.

You can expect to see many differences between a person's right and left hands. Some of the lines will be similar but others will vary dramatically.

Quick reminder

Dominant hand: *the hand you write with*

Nondominant hand: *the hand you do not write with*

HOW TO MAKE A RECORD OF THE PALM

When you start to practice palmistry you will quickly realize that you must find a practical way of recording the palms you have looked at. You will want to refer back to them, especially if you hope to become a serious palmist. For example, you might want to compare what you found in someone's palm a year ago with the state of the hand now, or chart the changes that you see in the hand of a growing child. It is very time-consuming to take laborious notes, and not even these will record every line and mark on the hand. The answer is either to photocopy the palm or take palm prints.

PHOTOCOPYING THE PALM

This is very simple if you have access to an ordinary photocopier. Simply place the palm face down and keep it still as the light beam passes over it. It is a good idea to have several practice runs in order to get the right amount of contrast in tone, because you do not want the copy to be too dark or too light.

TAKING A PALM PRINT

This process is not nearly as complicated, or as messy, as it sounds. However, it does take practice before you get it right, so do not give up if your initial attempts are not good enough. Make sure you use a water-based ink or paint, so that it is easy to remove it afterward.

Ask the person to wash his or her hands thoroughly to remove all traces of grease or dirt, as these will ruin the image. You should also politely ask for any jewelry to be taken off,

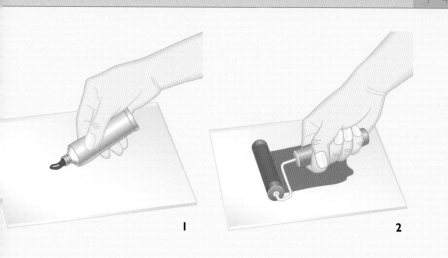

1

2

although a wedding ring may be kept on. You will need the following equipment:

- Good-quality paper large enough to take the whole palm print
- A thin pad of foam rubber
- A tube of water-based ink or watercolor paint
- A sheet of glass with bevelled edges or a sheet of linoleum
- A rubber roller about 4 inches (10 cm) wide
- A pen or pencil

1. Prepare everything before you begin. Place the sheet of paper over the pad of foam rubber, and put them both on a flat, firm surface. Squeeze a small amount of ink or paint on to the sheet of glass or linoleum.

2. Use the roller to distribute a thin, even layer of ink or paint over the glass or linoleum. Make sure there are no gaps or blobs, as these will ruin the clarity of the print.

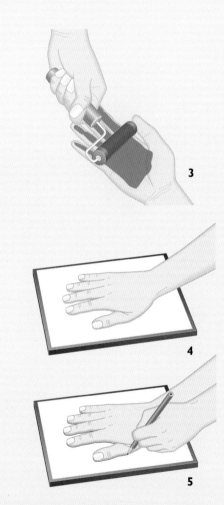

3. Run the roller over the ink or paint and then roll it over the person's palm. Always roll in one direction only. Roll down well past the wrist so that you capture any marks here as well.

4. Ask the person to place his or her palm flat on the paper, either while sitting or standing. He or she should keep the hand motionless while you press down on it gently to record the marks on the center of the palm.

5. If you wish, you can now trace around the outline of the person's hand with a pen or pencil. He or she should remove the hand while you hold down the edges of the paper. Repeat with the other hand and fresh paper.

Basic rules

Here are some simple rules to remember when you record a palm. If you always follow these guidelines you will create a good library of prints and cards containing all the information you need.

- Always take a print of both the right and left hands.
- Always write on each print whether it is the right or left hand, and whether it is the dominant hand.
- Do not forget to write the person's full name on each print, and the day, month and year of the reading.
- On a separate card, cross-indexed to the print, record biographical information about the person, including name, age, sex, marital status, number of children, occupation and anything else that is noteworthy.
- On the same card, add relevant palmistry information that is not shown in the hand print, such as the texture and feel of the skin, the flexibility of the fingers and hand, the knotty or smooth nature of the joints, and the shape and condition of the nails.

HOW WE GIVE OURSELVES AWAY

Body language has become one of the four branches of modern palmistry because the movements we make with our bodies reveal so much about us. People who are very skilled at reading body language will notice tiny nuances that escape the rest of us, but even so we can all discover a great deal about others by observing their actions during everyday encounters.

You probably already do this without realizing it. Noticing the behavior of your nearest and dearest tells you what sort of mood they are in. For instance, you may know that your partner tugs at his left ear when he is feeling anxious. You will also have your own collection of gestures that describe how you are feeling and what you are thinking.

BODY LANGUAGE AND PALMISTRY

When body language is applied to palmistry, the palmist takes note of every gesture that a client makes, as well as the way he sits in his chair. You can do the same. Is the person giving some sign of being nervous, such as fiddling with his clothes or twisting a ring round his finger? Is this a temporary state because he is slightly anxious about what the reading will tell him, or is he habitually nervous? Take a look at his fingers. Does he bite his nails or chew the sides of his fingers?

How does that person hold his hands before you start the reading? Are they relaxed or clenched? If he has made fists of his hands, what are

his thumbs doing? If they are hidden inside his fingers it shows that he is anxious and defensive. If the thumbs are tucked around the outside of the fingers, he is feeling combative. If his hands are completely out of sight, perhaps in his pockets, or he has his

We continually reveal our thoughts and feelings through our body language.

arms crossed with his hands deep in his armpits, he is reluctant to give anything away and you will have to win him over.

HOW TO GIVE A RESPONSIBLE READING

What do you do when you want to give someone a palmistry reading? The first and most important point to remember is to take it gently and choose your words carefully. The person whose hands you are reading will be listening intently to you and will place tremendous importance on your words, even if she appears to be treating the whole thing as a joke. So it is very important to be a responsible palmist and to consider the other person's feelings throughout.

FEARS

Some people have deep-seated fears about having their palms read, even if they are reluctant to admit it. For instance, someone might have resisted having her palm read for years because she is scared that the palmist will give

her some terrible news or tell her when she is going to die. She may still be harboring these fears when you offer to read her palms, and will be

When giving someone a reading, be sensitive to their mood and possible fears.

listening for the tiniest suggestion that something ghastly is going to happen to her.

As a result, you must be very careful about what you convey through your tone of voice and body language. Do not look startled when you see her hands, or gasp, mutter to yourself, fidget or do anything else that suggests that you are worried. Even if you are seriously concerned by what you see in

Do your best to create a good rapport with the other person so she can relax.

her hands, you must find a tactful way of saying so. If you think she is heading for a health crisis, do not immediately tell her to see a doctor or face the consequences. Choose your words very carefully and approach the subject with tact. You could say that it looks as though she has been feeling

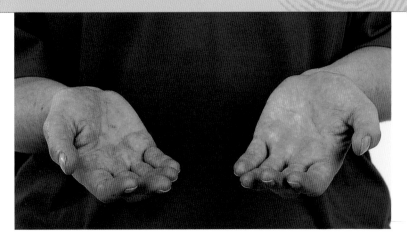

tired lately, and suggest that she has a medical check-up if things do not improve. However, do not be alarmist. There are many stories of people being scared stiff by irresponsible palmists who have baldly prophesied serious illness or even death. Do not become one of them!

POWER

If you have ever watched people giving you important news, you will have noticed that very often they look rather pleased with themselves, because being first with the news makes them

When someone shows you their palms they are placing their trust in you.

feel important. There are some palmists who behave in the same way and who feel big or special because of their skills. This means that they have a lot of ego invested in what they do, so they behave as though they are superior in some way. Try to resist the very human temptation to act like this yourself, even if the other person's conversation is full of compliments about how clever you are. Perhaps he always gushes when he feels nervous, so all those fine words about your wonderful skills are really a defense mechanism against his anxiety. Thank him for the compliments, but do not let them go to your head.

I AM THE PALMIST AND I AM ALWAYS RIGHT

This is a trap that even experienced palmists can fall into, so do your best to resist it from the start. In fact, it is a pitfall for all those who consider themselves to be experts in their chosen field, ranging from medicine to cooking and everything in between. If you want to be a skilled, sensitive palmist you must accept the fact that sometimes you will get things wrong. We are all fallible; it is part of being human. Yes, it can be unnerving if the other person disagrees with what you say during a reading, because it almost always makes you doubt your own skills, but do not start arguing with him about who is right. It might help to rephrase what you have said, because perhaps you were not clear the first time round. If you describe an incident from someone's past and he denies that such a thing happened, suggest politely that he mull over your

This man's reluctance to reveal his palms means he is not being open.

words later on, because he might remember an incident that relates to what you have said. After that, drop the subject and carry on with the rest of the reading.

DENIAL

Even though you will sometimes be told that you have got something wrong, that may not necessarily be true. Perhaps you have hit the nail on the head with such accuracy that the other person cannot bear to admit it. Maybe you have touched on something that terrifies her, so she denies its existence. You must respect this, especially if you are not a trained psychotherapist or counselor, and not insist that she face up to things she is not yet ready to tackle.

IS SILENCE GOLDEN?

Imagine you are reading your best friend's palm. You dislike her new partner and have heard rumors about

Watch someone's hand gestures during the reading to see how he is feeling.

what he gets up to behind your friend's back, and one glance at your friend's heart line confirms your worst fears. Should you say something or keep quiet? This depends on the circumstances and your conscience, but do be very careful if you feel duty-bound to speak up, because friendships have often been ruined by this sort of situation. Your friend may ditch you and keep her partner, even if she later regrets it.

What you must never do is allow your own opinions or prejudices to color your readings, or use a reading as an opportunity to give someone a piece of your mind. You may think you know exactly what your friend should do with her life (such as give up what you believe is her crazy dream of becoming an actress and retrain for a proper job with a decent pension), but you should be very wary of saying so. These are your opinions and they have nothing to do with palmistry. Even if you think your friend's hand shows she is not cut out for the acting profession, ask yourself if you are simply seeing what you

want to see. Palmistry is not an excuse to tell someone how to live her life, no matter how well-meaning your intentions may be.

Face-to-face readings allow you to establish and maintain strong eye contact.

Ideally, you should give readings seated at a table and in good, natural light.

BEFORE THE READING

Now that you know some of the pitfalls connected with readings, you are ready to start giving your own. Ideally, you should prepare yourself for each reading by doing the grounding exercise given on the right, as this will help you to center yourself. If this is not possible, even a couple of minutes spent doing some deep breathing will be helpful.

Grounding exercise

Sit quietly by yourself, with both feet on the floor, and take some deep, relaxing breaths. Clear your mind of chatter. Imagine a shower of white light falling around you, cleansing any negative thoughts. Then imagine that roots are growing out of the soles of your feet deep into the earth, and that a beam of light is connecting the top of your head with the spirit realms. Ask for guidance and protection during the reading. You are now ready to begin.

If you are giving the reading in a room in your home, make sure it is clean, tidy and smells fresh. And the same goes for you, too! Check that there is plenty of light so you can see the person's hands clearly, and make sure his chair is comfortable. If you would like him to place his hands on a table during the reading, make sure the table is at the right height for him, so he will not feel uncomfortable.

DURING THE READING

As well as remembering all the advice you have already read, there are other points to consider as well.

Before you start the reading, you should ask the person how old she is. Explain that you need this information to discover at what stage she is in her life by finding her current age on each line in her hand. For instance, if you can see that a major event takes place when she is about 40, you need to know whether

she has already experienced this or whether it is still to come.

After this, try to limit your questions to whatever is relevant. If you ask too many questions, the person may think you are fishing for information that you will then repeat back to her at a later stage. However, there is nothing wrong in describing what you see and then asking a question based on your findings.

Essential equipment for a reading

- *Comfortable chairs for both you and your client.*
- *A good source of light, preferably including an adjustable-neck lamp.*
- *A magnifying glass to enable you to examine the hands in detail.*

Sitting side-by-side for a reading creates an intimate, confiding atmosphere.

For example, if you are looking at the hand of a born teacher, you could say so and then ask if she has any teaching experience or has ever wanted to be a teacher. This is much more impressive than asking what she does for a living and then saying that you can see her chosen profession in her hand.

How long should your readings take? At first your readings will be short because you will probably feel rather self-conscious and will wonder what to say. As you gain in confidence,

Washing your hands cleanses your energy after a difficult or stressful reading.

you will find more to talk about, at which point you should decide in advance how long each reading will last. Usually anything over one hour becomes tiring—not just for you, but for the other person as well, because you are both concentrating so hard.

You should also think about whether to tape the readings. Recording the session is another

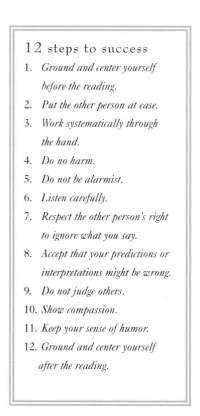

reason for the client to feel self-conscious at first, but it does mean she will have a record of the reading to listen to later on. It saves her having to struggle to remember everything you told her, so that she can relax and enjoy the session.

AFTER THE READING

It is enjoyable and satisfying to give readings, but they can also be very tiring because of all the effort involved. Just as you grounded yourself before the reading began, so it is important to ground yourself again after the session is over: sit quietly by yourself and imagine a shower of white light falling over you, then repeat the exercise, picturing roots growing out of the soles of your feet into the earth.

If the reading was difficult for some reason, perhaps because it stirred up a lot of emotion in the other person, you may want to cleanse the atmosphere. You might already have a favorite

12 steps to success

1. *Ground and center yourself before the reading.*
2. *Put the other person at ease.*
3. *Work systematically through the hand.*
4. *Do no harm.*
5. *Do not be alarmist.*
6. *Listen carefully.*
7. *Respect the other person's right to ignore what you say.*
8. *Accept that your predictions or interpretations might be wrong.*
9. *Do not judge others.*
10. *Show compassion.*
11. *Keep your sense of humor.*
12. *Ground and center yourself after the reading.*

method of doing this, but if not you could clap your hands or use a singing bowl to dispel the negative energy.

PALMISTRY DIRECTORY

The directory teaches you the nuts and bolts of palmistry, starting with the basic shapes of the hands and working up to the meanings of the individual lines. It then shows you how to draw on this essential information to read people's palms and discover their characters.

Start slowly so that you can build up your knowledge in stages, and then you will find it easier to remember what you read. You can practice your skills whenever you are with other people, simply by glancing at their hands and analyzing what you see. You will soon realize that you have a fascinating and valuable new skill that will help you in every area of your life, from understanding your family to knowing whether you can trust the mechanic who looks after your car. As well as learning about other people, you will also discover a wealth of information about yourself, including your creative potential and attitude to romance.

HOW TO USE THE DIRECTORY

This part of the book has been specially designed to help you build up your understanding of palmistry step-by-step. If you work through the directory systematically you will gain a solid foundation of knowledge, from the basics right through to more complex information. It explores the following topics:

- **First impressions** (see pages 48–63) This section takes you through the initial stages of a reading, and helps you tune in to the energy of the person whose hand you are reading.
- **The hand** (see pages 64–97) Here you are introduced to the four basic hand shapes and the different mounts on the palm.

It is important to study the overall shape and texture of someone's hand.

- **The fingers and thumbs** (see pages 98–137) In this section you will learn how to examine the fingers and thumbs in detail.

- **The lines of the hand** (see pages 138–249) This part of the book

Our hands describe our capacity and willingness to form close relationships.

describes the role of each of the major lines in the hand, as well as many of the minor ones. You will

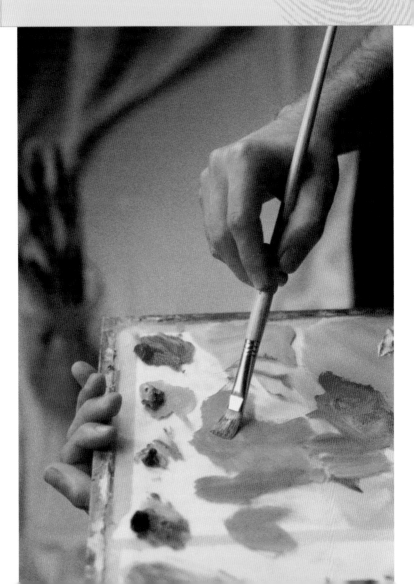

also discover how to time the events shown on the lines of the hand.

- **Love and relationships** (see pages 250–283) This section shows you how to detect someone's emotional make-up from the lines and shape of the hand. You can also study your own hand to discover your capacity for romance and passion.
- **Ambition and career** (see pages 284–309) Here you will learn how to read people's career potential. Do they have entrepreneurial skills? Will they ultimately be successful? You will be able to answer all these questions about yourself, too.
- **Talents and abilities** (see pages 310–339) This section will help you learn more about your own skills and it is equally helpful if a friend or loved one wants to know what to do with his life.

The shapes and lines of our hands describe our talents and potential.

> ### Your palmistry toolkit
> - *Index cards for writing down your thoughts and ideas.*
> - *Pen or pencil.*
> - *Equipment for making palm prints (see page 26).*
> - *Magnifying glass.*
> - *A good light, such as an adjustable-angle lamp.*
> - *Tape recorder and tapes for recording your readings.*

- **Temperaments** (see pages 340–381) This will tell you if someone has a filthy temper, prefers her own company, is a pessimist or can never keep hold of her money.

FIRST IMPRESSIONS

Never dismiss your first impressions of someone. They are invaluable because your brain is registering all sorts of information about the other person, from the size of his pupils to his smell. You are also interpreting many subconscious signals, such as his body language. And he, of course, is noting exactly the same things about you.

If you can train yourself to be aware of some of these first impressions, they will be very useful when you start to read palms. If you always greet someone by shaking his hand, notice what happens. Does he give you a firm handshake that shows he is open and friendly? Does he give you a bone-crusher handshake that is intended to be macho and dominant, although in reality it shows an inferiority complex? Or does he give you a wet-fish handshake, which suggests that he has no desire to meet you at all?

THE NATURAL HAND POSITION

A palmistry reading starts long before you begin your detailed examination of someone's palms. Ask the person in question to settle herself in her chair and then to hold out her hands. You are about to discover some vital information about her, but you must resist saying so because you will make her feel self-conscious.

Do not give her any instructions about how to hold her hands at this stage. All this will come later, but right now you want to know her natural hand position. It will tell you about her innate character, whether she is generous or guarded, open or shy, easy to know or elusive.

THE CLOSED HAND

If she holds out her hand with her thumb touching one of her fingers, she is showing a closed hand. She is instinctively hiding half of her palm, which indicates that a large part of her personality is also under wraps. This is

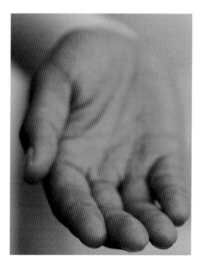

This person's thumb is held close to the rest of his hand, showing caution.

the sort of person whom you can know for years without her ever really opening up to you with true intimacy, because part of her is always closed off from everyone.

THE OPEN HAND

If she holds out her hand with her thumb held away from her fingers, she is showing an open hand. This is the reverse of the closed hand, because she is opening herself up to you by displaying her palm. Such a person is friendly and approachable. However, you do not yet know the whole story and must now look closely at the amount of space between the sides of her hands and her thumbs.

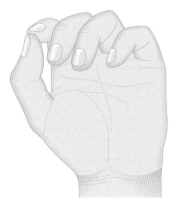

When a person's thumb touches his index finger he is showing a closed hand.

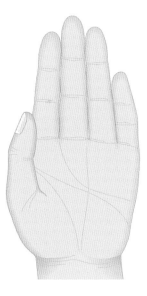

When the thumb is held next to the hand, the person is closed off from others.

THE ANGLE OF THE THUMB

Look carefully at each hand to discover the angle formed by the thumb and index finger. It indicates her level of generosity and open-mindedness—the bigger the angle, the more generous and open the person. Look at the angle on each hand in turn, because it is quite common to find that one is bigger than the other. For instance, someone

Always look at the angle between the thumb and the side of the hand. In this example it is a normal angle because it is between 45 and 90 degrees.

who is right-handed may hold her left thumb nearer to her index finger than her right thumb. This shows someone who is instinctively cautious, both emotionally and financially (the narrow angle on her left hand), but who has learned to overcome these reservations and be more open (the wider angle on her right hand).

When you find the reverse—the narrowest angle on the dominant hand—that person's instincts are to be much more open than she actually allows herself to be. Such reservations may have been caused by a succession of unpleasant experiences in which others took her for granted, so she has learned to protect herself by giving less away over the years, whether financially or emotionally.

HOW BIG IS THE ANGLE?

So far you have only noticed whether the angle on one hand is larger than that on the other. The next stage is to assess the actual size of each angle between the thumb and index finger.

Do not let the person move her hands yet, otherwise you will lose this all-important information. Looking at each hand in turn, judge the size of the angle between the thumb and index finger. Anything between 45 and 90 degrees is considered normal and belongs to someone who has an average emotional temperament.

If the angle is smaller than this, she is narrow-minded, self-centered and emotionally closed off to the rest of the world. The lack of space between her thumb and index finger reflects a lack of space in her life for other people. Of course, you will have to choose your words carefully when saying this to her. If the angle is larger than 90 degrees, you are looking at the hand of someone who is a born leader, and emotionally generous with it. She is open to experiences and ready to tackle whatever comes her way.

WHAT THE HAND LOOKS AND FEELS LIKE

At this stage you are still absorbing your initial impressions of someone's hand. So far you have observed the way he holds his hands when feeling relaxed, which will have told you whether he is naturally open-minded or rather reserved and cautious. You are now ready to look at the hand in more detail and assess what it actually feels like.

LOOKING AT THE PALMS

The person should still be holding his palms out in front of you, so take the opportunity to examine them. Remember, you are not looking at the fingers or lines in detail at this stage; you are simply adding to your first impressions of his hands.

What do you notice about the palms? Are they calloused, suggesting

Spend time examining the hand in detail. At this stage you are looking at its overall shape, firmness and texture.

that he does a lot of work with his hands, or so smooth that it looks as though someone else does all the hard work for him? You may not notice if the hands are clean, but it will certainly register if they are grubby. If so, ask yourself why he has not bothered to wash his hands before having them examined. Take a look at his clothes and hair. Are these dirty too, suggesting that he has slovenly habits or wants to make a rebellious statement about himself?

THE SPACES BETWEEN THE FINGERS

While his palms are spread out in front of you, check whether his fingers are held together or apart. If the fingers are spread out, he has a generous and receptive nature. If the fingers are held together, he is practical and cautious with money. It is as though he is holding his fingers together so that nothing valuable can slip through.

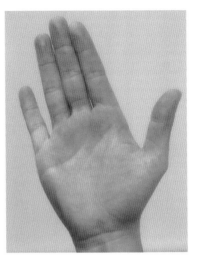

Look for any noticeable gaps between the fingers when the hand is resting.

LOOKING AT THE BACKS OF THE HANDS

Before you go any further, explain to him that you are now going to hold his hands and ask him if this is all right. It is important always to give advance warning that you are going to touch someone, in case the person is very nervous or anxious about what you are doing. It also helps to guard against any possibility of him misinterpreting your actions and reacting with embarrassment.

Work with one hand at a time. Gently take the hand in yours and turn it over so that you can examine the nails and the back of the hand. What do they look like? Do any thoughts or impressions come to you? Allow your intuition to start flowing as you look at the hands.

THE FEEL OF THE HANDS

Now that you are holding the person's hands in yours, how do they feel? Are they very cool to the touch, nicely warm or very hot? If they are very cool, this may be because he is nervous or cold. Or is there another reason, such as poor circulation? This might be something to mention to him, but only in passing, and you should certainly not give medical diagnoses or scare

him. Hot hands belong to someone with a fast metabolism who burns up the body's energy very quickly.

You need to study the hand from every angle, including from the side.

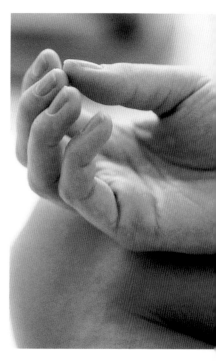

If the hands are very dry, is that because they are neglected? Why do you think this might be? Very clammy hands are a classic sign of nervousness, so you could check them again later in the reading when, with luck, the person has calmed down and is feeling more relaxed.

LOOKING AT THE NAILS

Are the nails in good condition? If they are well cared for, the person takes pride in his appearance. Dirty or broken nails tell the opposite story, unless the person in question has a physical job or pastime, such as gardening, that would explain the condition of his nails. Very long nails suggest an impractical person, because it is almost impossible to carry out many domestic tasks with such nails. Here is another piece of the jigsaw that is forming a fuller picture of this person's character.

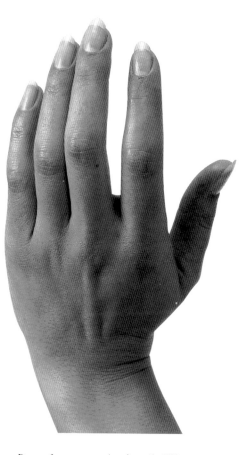

Do not forget to examine the nails. This woman obviously cares for hers.

SKIN MARKINGS

FINGERPRINTS

Take a good look at the skin on your fingertips. You will probably need to do this under a strong light, and possibly with a magnifying glass. Alternatively, take clear prints of your own hands and then examine them at your leisure; this may be more comfortable than holding your hands in the air for long periods.

Fingerprints are divided into three main types: arches, whorls and loops. There are two variations as well: tented arches and composite whorls. Look at each finger in turn and then count up the number of fingerprints of each type to establish which one dominates the personality. If you have found a majority of one type of pattern, but a couple of fingers have different patterns, you can easily interpret these by combining the meaning of the pattern with the meaning of the finger.

Arches

These indicate a practical, reliable and trustworthy personality. This person is clever with her hands and may have a job that involves making things. She is grounded and realistic, but can be stubborn, especially in the face of change. This can mean she is reluctant to make big alterations to her life.

This is an arched fingerprint. The shape of the arch itself can vary, either being fairly flat or very rounded.

Whorls

Someone with lots of whorls on her fingertips is extraordinary in some way. She may have a special skill, or might have devoted her life to a particular cause, and treads her own path through life rather than following someone else's lead. She is highly individualistic, which can set her apart from others. These traits are accentuated if the whorl is set high up on the finger, nearer the top of the finger than the base of the first phalange (or section).

In a whorl the lines curl round each other in rings. A majority of whorls shows someone who can be stubborn.

Loops

Loops show an easy-going and sociable person. She is tactful and fits in well with others, and is good at reaching compromises when necessary. She prefers to go with the flow rather than stand out from the crowd, which sometimes make her popular, but at other times can reduce her individuality.

In a loop fingerprint, the loop can be formed from the right or left.

A tented arch is similar to an arch but its shape is much more exaggerated.

A composite whorl consists of two loop patterns wrapped around each other.

Tented arches

These look like ordinary arches, but have a little vertical line in the middle of the arch. Tented arches have the same basic meaning as ordinary arches, but indicate much more enthusiasm about life. This person is also much more receptive to change than someone with ordinary arches.

Composite whorls

You will know when you are looking at a composite whorl because you will see two loops wrapped around each other. A composite whorl has a similar meaning to an ordinary whorl, but also shows someone who sees two sides to every story. This trait can be very useful, but it can also make the person indecisive.

PALM PRINTS

Unique markings are not restricted to our fingertips, because you will find other patterns on the palms when you look at them closely. These are formed

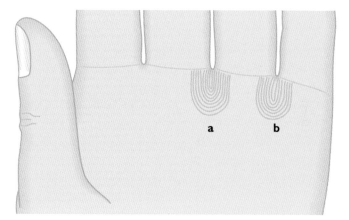

by skin ridges, and some of them are particularly interesting because not everyone has them.

Loop of seriousness

Look for this loop between the Saturn and Apollo mounts (see pages 80–83). If it is present, it shows someone who is driven by a particular goal, especially if it appears on both hands; in this case the person will end up devoting her whole life to this all-consuming interest.

DIFFERENT LOOPS
a *Loop of seriousness*
b *Loop of humor*

Loop of humor

This loop appears between the Apollo and Mercury fingers (see pages 130–137). It shows someone who is optimistic and has a sense of humor. She is cheerful, popular and very diplomatic.

THE THREE WORLDS

It is a useful exercise to divide the palm up into these three sections, because it allows you to study each section in turn without being distracted by what happens above or below it. If you are looking at just one segment, you will automatically screen off the rest of the hand.

THE IDEAL WORLD

This part of the hand covers the tops of the fingers down to the point where they meet the palm. It describes someone's hopes and wishes, and his intellectual and spiritual interests. Look carefully at this part of the hand to see its level of development. Are the fingers strong and well formed? Now compare it with the other two sections of the hand. If this is the longest or strongest part, it shows that the person enjoys using his brain and has a deep interest in spiritual matters.

THE PRACTICAL WORLD

The practical section of the hand runs from the base of the fingers to the bottom of the two mounts of Mars. If it is the largest part, or the most well defined, it shows that the person is able to operate on a practical level, perhaps by running a successful business or simply by managing his everyday affairs with competence and efficiency.

THE MATERIAL WORLD

The material world is represented by the lowest section of the hand, running from the base of the mounts of Mars down to the wrist. It includes the thumb, which is a very important part of the hand. Is this the strongest of the three sections? If so, it indicates that this person is driven by basic instincts and desires, such as his need for financial and emotional security. He may be reluctant to take risks.

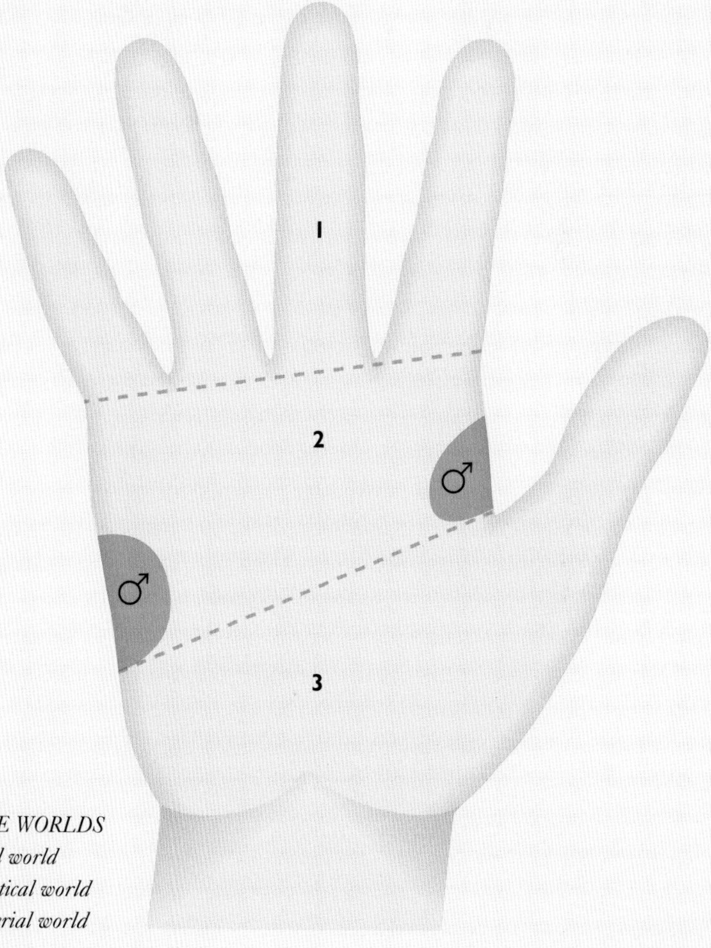

THREE WORLDS
1 *Ideal world*
2 *Practical world*
3 *Material world*

THE HAND

You can tell a lot about a person simply by looking at the shape of the hands. Even without a detailed analysis of the lines and markings on the palm, the shape and proportions of the hand and fingers, the edge of the palm and a hand's contours or "mounts" can all give you instant insights into someone's basic personality.

In this section of the book you will learn to recognize the four basic hand shapes: the fire, earth, air and water hands. You can practice your ability to identify them by looking at the hands of your friends and family. Does your best friend have the same hand shape as you, or is it very different? Look at the hands of the people you see on television, such as film stars, politicians and actors. Are they what you would have expected to see, or do their hands tell a different story from the personality they are projecting?

ASSESSING THE HAND SHAPE

What do you look for when you want to assess the shape of someone's hand? The traditional method is to divide hands into seven shapes: elementary, square, conic, spatulate, psychic, philosophic and mixed. However, this can be complicated because there is so much information to remember about each shape. The modern approach is to divide hands into four shapes that are based on the four astrological elements: fire, earth, air and water. This does not mean that someone belonging to one of the earth signs of Taurus, Virgo or Capricorn invariably has an earth hand, because life is not that simple. Nevertheless, if you know the person's Sun sign, it will be interesting to see whether it corresponds to the hand shape or whether these are very different.

Not all hands correspond exactly to one of the four shapes, so at times you

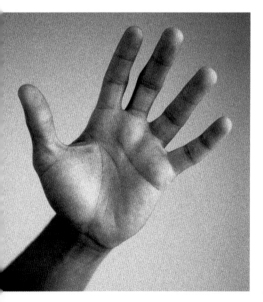

This is a typical fire hand, with a long palm and relatively short fingers.

Take time to assess a person's hand shape at the start of the reading.

If you are new to palmistry you will probably be eager to get started on the exciting business of studying the lines on someone's hands, or those on your own hands. It is tempting to miss out some of the foundation stages of reading a hand (such as looking at the shape of the hand), because these seem rather basic. However, if you ignore these steps you will lack important pieces of information, which could help you draw more significance from the lines when you come to read them. For instance, if you are studying a palm that is covered with many fine lines, it is important to know which hand shape it belongs to. You would expect to see these lines if you were looking at a water hand, but they would be unusual in an earth hand and would give you important information about the person in question.

will have to use your own judgment, perhaps based on the number of subsidiary lines on the palm, or the texture and resilience of the skin, before making up your mind.

THE FIRE HAND

SHAPE Long palm, with fingers shorter than the palm

SKIN Firm, warm and springy

NUMBER OF LINES Major and minor lines clearly marked

OTHER INDICATIONS Fingers may be spatulate

PERSONALITY Energetic, impulsive, sense of adventure

The element of fire rules enthusiasm, intuition and energy. It is always looking for new outlets and methods of expression.

MAIN CHARACTERISTICS

This is someone who is buzzing with energy. She is impulsive and enthusiastic, adventurous and receptive. She finds it difficult to relax because there is always something she wants to do and she prefers to be fully occupied. It may even be difficult to get her to sit still long enough for you to read her palm.

Ideally, she should lead an active life and get plenty of exercise in the fresh air, as this gives her the opportunity to burn off the excess nervous energy that she often accumulates. If she does not have this sort of outlet, she can become frustrated and rather irritable. Nevertheless, she must take care not to wear herself out by skimping on rest or sleep, as she has a tendency to

A typical fire hand has a long, rectangular palm. The fingers are slightly shorter than the palm. The hand feels springy.

burn the candle at both ends. She can also sometimes eat and drink to excess, and physical exercise will help to counteract this.

ACTIVITIES

Someone with a fire hand is a born performer and invariably ends up holding the stage at social gatherings. She may be drawn to one of the performing arts or to some other career in which she can take control and be in the spotlight. This person is naturally competitive and is always looking for a challenge: a tendency that will be increased if she was born under the fire sign of Aries, Leo or Sagittarius. She is an excellent leader and organizer, as her instincts tell her to take charge of situations.

THE EARTH HAND

SHAPE Square palm and short fingers

SKIN Thick, possibly coarse, with a hard palm

NUMBER OF LINES Major lines strongly marked, but few minor lines and sometimes none at all

OTHER INDICATIONS Fingers and joints are fairly stiff

PERSONALITY Capable, helpful, reliable, honest

The earth element rules practical and material matters and is grounded in reality. It is connected with continuity and stability.

MAIN CHARACTERISTICS

This is someone who is helpful and reliable, and who may spend a lot of time giving practical assistance to others. For instance, he may be the first port of call when others are dealing with household emergencies.

He has plenty of common sense, but may find it difficult to cope with open displays of emotion.

He is loyal and honest and, unless there are indications to the contrary, uncomplicated, too. To a large extent, what you see is what you get, because it would not occur to him to disguise his feelings or motives, especially if he was born under one of the earth signs of Taurus, Virgo or Capricorn. As a result he may feel bemused when

A classic earth hand has a square palm and fingers that are slightly shorter than the palm. The flesh is firm.

or pottery. He can also make a good surgeon because he is so grounded, unflustered and knows how to concentrate on the essentials. He has a strong attraction to nature, enjoys being in the open air and has the potential to be a good gardener. He is happier leading a rural life than one that is urban, and has a good affinity with animals. If he lives in a city, he will enjoy tending his own patch of greenery, even if it is only a modest window box or house plant.

confronted by someone who is not always straightforward.

ACTIVITIES

Someone with an earth hand can be very creative, and is drawn to activities that primarily involve making things with his hands, such as wood carving

THE AIR HAND

SHAPE Square palm, long fingers

SKIN Dry, and the hand feels soft when pressed

NUMBER OF LINES Major lines clearly marked, but the lines are quite thin

OTHER INDICATIONS Fingers and joints are flexible

PERSONALITY Intelligent, logical and good at communicating

The air element rules the mental processes, such as thinking and talking, and creates a strong urge to communicate thoughts and ideas.

MAIN CHARACTERISTICS

Someone with an air hand lives mainly in her mind. She enjoys using her brain, not only for work but for pleasure, and is usually intelligent. She is logical and likes to think things through for herself, rather than be told what to do or say. She is someone who excels at all forms of communication, especially if she was born under one of the air signs of Gemini, Libra or Aquarius. She will happily take part in discussions and conversations in which she can share her ideas with like-minded people.

However, she gets uncomfortable when dealing with emotions. She prefers to talk about and analyze her feelings rather than experience them, especially when faced with an emotional problem. When this

In an air hand, you will see a square palm and fingers that are slightly longer than the palm. The skin feels dry.

happens it may help her to record her thoughts in a journal, to give her an outlet for her emotions.

ACTIVITIES
Such a cerebral existence means that it is important for someone with an air hand to get plenty of exercise, although it will bore her unless she has a friend to keep her company. She thrives on a busy schedule and is best suited to a career that involves some form of intellectual pressure, such as journalism or teaching. Boredom threatens whenever she lacks mental stimulation, and this applies to relationships as well: she needs a lively partner who will keep her on her toes intellectually.

THE WATER HAND

SHAPE Long palm and long fingers

SKIN Damp and soft

NUMBER OF LINES Major lines thinly marked, with many thin lines running across the palm

OTHER INDICATIONS May have a limp handshake

PERSONALITY Sensitive, emotional, unworldly, intuitive

The water element rules the emotions and the intuition. It is connected with spiritual matters and creativity.

MAIN CHARACTERISTICS

This is someone who lives through his emotions and is easily hurt. He will be even more sensitive if he was born under one of the water signs of Cancer, Scorpio or Pisces. He can tune in to the atmosphere around him, picking up other people's moods or the feel of a house. He says he cannot explain his impressions, but just "knows" they are right. It is hard for him to keep both feet on the ground because he lives in a world of his own, ruled by sensitivity, heightened emotion and a powerful imagination.

Someone with a water hand can be very unworldly and trusting, with the unfortunate result that he is taken for granted by those who look on him as easy prey. It is important for him to

When looking at a water hand you will see a long, rectangular palm and fingers that are longer than the palm. The skin is soft.

have some form of spiritual belief or practice, otherwise he can feel that something important is missing from his life. He should take care with his health because he may lack physical stamina and is easily drained of energy by difficult situations.

ACTIVITIES

This person is extremely creative and may be drawn to the arts, such as painting, dancing or music. However, he is unlikely to be practical: He can write a poem, but has no idea how to rewire an electrical plug. He is capable of great compassion, so is attracted to counseling or the healing professions, although he may be more interested in complementary therapies than in allopathic medicine.

THE MOUNTS
OF THE HAND

WHERE   The fleshy pads that lie at the base of the
fingers and thumbs, and on the edges of the palm

INDICATE   Vitality and enjoyment of life

The mount under each finger is named after that finger, so the mount under the index or Jupiter finger is called the mount of Jupiter, and so on. The mount at the base of the thumb is called the mount of Venus, and lies opposite the mount of the Moon. The middle of the palm is ruled by Mars: There are two mounts of Mars and the center of the palm is known as the plain of Mars. To see all the mounts, hold the fingers together with the palm slightly cupped, then look sideways at the palm; the mounts may be soft or hard in texture.

WELL-DEVELOPED MOUNTS
As a general rule, the higher the mounts are on a hand, the more enthusiastic and vibrant that person is.

THIN AND FLAT MOUNTS
If the mounts on the hand are flat, as though they have been ironed out, that person has a low-key, slightly disinterested attitude to life.

MISSING MOUNTS
Not every hand has every mount, and in some cases you will find that two mounts have merged together.

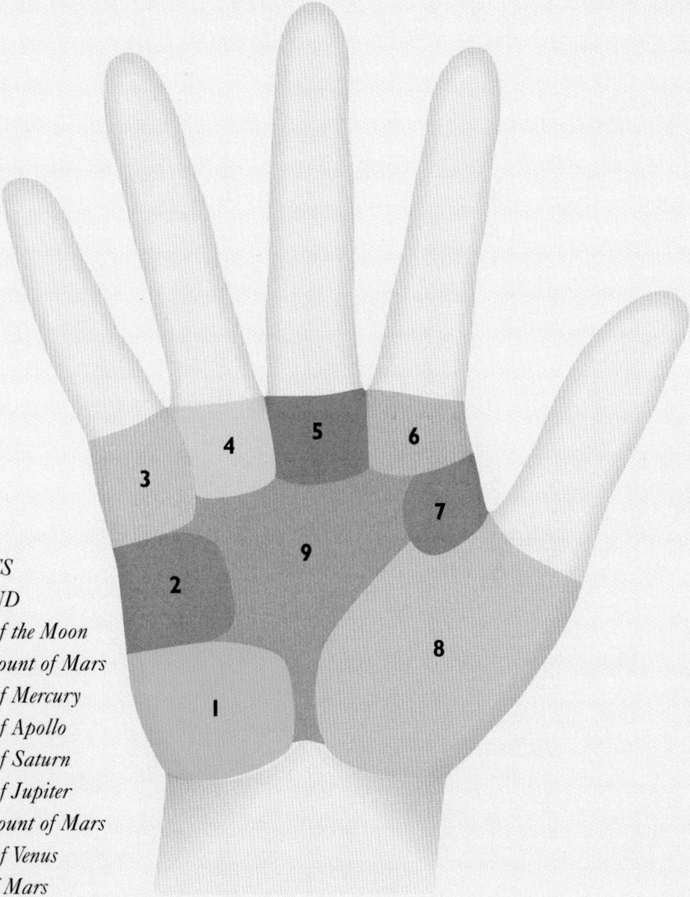

THE MOUNTS
OF THE HAND

1 ☽ *Mount of the Moon*
2 ♂ *Outer mount of Mars*
3 ☿ *Mount of Mercury*
4 ☉ *Mount of Apollo*
5 ♄ *Mount of Saturn*
6 ♃ *Mount of Jupiter*
7 ♂ *Inner mount of Mars*
8 ♀ *Mount of Venus*
9 ♂ *Plain of Mars*

THE MOUNT OF JUPITER

WHERE The fleshy pad that lies beneath the index or Jupiter finger

INDICATES Ambition, leadership ability, confidence and hunger for success

In astrology, Jupiter is the planet that rules expansion, optimism, prosperity and luck. It also rules confidence and joviality.

NORMAL

A mount of Jupiter that is easily identified and of normal size (neither too prominent nor too flat) indicates someone with good leadership qualities, who is not afraid to use them. He is sociable, friendly,

A thick Jupiter finger and a large Jupiter mount show arrogance and conceit.

confident and popular, with a healthy level of ambition.

OVERDEVELOPED

If the Jupiter mount is excessively large and fleshy, he may be confident to the point of being arrogant and controlling. Since he is convinced that his opinions are correct, he can be overbearing, bigoted and narrow-minded. These tendencies are increased if the Jupiter finger is the most dominant digit on his hand. A large mount of Jupiter coupled with a large inner mount of Mars directly beneath it suggests someone who is a bully.

THIN AND FLAT

A mount of Jupiter that is thin or hard to see indicates someone who lacks confidence and likes other people to take the lead, especially if the Jupiter finger is short. He does not have many ambitions and allows himself to be carried along by life.

Expert tip

If you cannot find the mount of Jupiter it may have merged with the mount of Saturn. In this case, you must combine the meanings of the two mounts. A Jupiter-Saturn mount indicates someone who is ambitious and confident, with the practical ability to achieve his goals. He also knows when holding back is the best strategy.

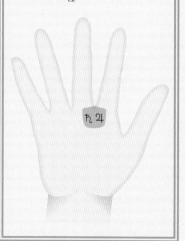

THE MOUNT OF SATURN

WHERE The fleshy pad that lies beneath the middle or Saturn finger

INDICATES Balance, resilience, responsibility and self-control

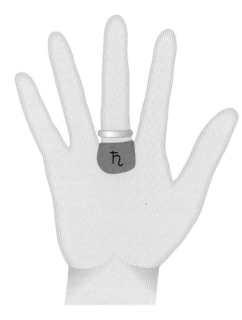

In astrology, Saturn is the planet of responsibility, limitations, pessimism and hard work. It also rules structure, boundaries and time.

NORMAL

A mount of Saturn that is of normal size, rather than being too flat or too big, denotes someone who has a well-balanced attitude to life. She is responsible and capable, and you can rely on her. She has plenty of common

A big Saturn mount and a ring on the Saturn finger show over-responsibility.

sense and a good sense of humor. She is not afraid of hard work and prefers to be left alone to get on with it.

OVERDEVELOPED

If the mount of Saturn is very pronounced, she has an equally developed sense of duty, which she may take to extremes. For instance, she may lead a rather Cinderella-like existence in which other people have all the fun while she is left behind to do the chores. Perhaps unsurprisingly, she is cynical and pessimistic.

THIN AND FLAT

Someone with a very flat mount of Saturn has little sense of responsibility, preferring to let others take care of the practical necessities of life. It may be hard for her to hold down a job because she does not seem to care about such things. These tendencies are accentuated if she has a short Saturn finger and/or a faint fate line.

Expert tip

If the mount seems very flat, check that it has not merged with either the Jupiter or Apollo mounts. A Jupiter-Saturn mount indicates someone who is ambitious, with the confidence and practicality to achieve her goals. A Saturn mount that has merged with the mount of Apollo shows someone who is practical and artistic.

THE MOUNT OF APOLLO

WHERE The fleshy pad that lies beneath the ring or Apollo finger

INDICATES Artistic ability, a sociable and convivial nature

Apollo was the Sun god of the Romans and therefore has close links with the Sun in astrology. The Sun rules our creative instincts, our identity and our journey through life.

NORMAL

Someone with a well-developed mount of Apollo, which is neither too large nor too small, is likely to be popular and gregarious. This person is good fun. He will appreciate beautiful things and, as a rule, has style and good taste. He has creative and artistic potential.

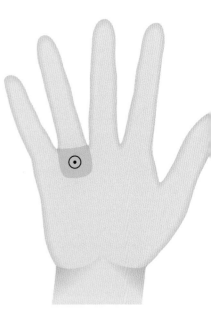

OVERDEVELOPED

An over-large mount of Apollo indicates someone who is showy, perhaps to the point of ostentation. These traits are emphasized if the mount of Jupiter or the Jupiter finger is also exaggerated. He enjoys being the center of attention and will try to steal the show if he finds himself out of the limelight. Conversations with him tend to revolve around his favorite subject—himself.

THIN AND FLAT

If the mount of Apollo is small or thin, he has little artistic talent or appreciation. He will not show much interest in outward appearances or in surrounding himself with beautiful objects. He may also have a rather dreary, prosaic personality that seems to lack color and sparkle.

A big Apollo mount and a long Jupiter finger indicate a tendency to show off.

Expert tip

Sometimes the mount of Apollo has blended with one of the mounts on either side of it. A Saturn-Apollo mount indicates someone who is creative and has the practical abilities to make the most of his talents. An Apollo-Mercury mount shows a person who has a way with words and who may make his living from communicating with others. He may also have lovely handwriting.

THE MOUNT OF MERCURY

WHERE The fleshy pad or mount that lies beneath the little or Mercury finger

INDICATES The ability to communicate with others, not only on a day-to-day level but also in business

In astrology, the planet Mercury rules communication and our ability to think. It is also connected with trickery and sharp practice.

NORMAL

A normal-sized mount of Mercury shows someone who finds it easy to connect with others. She is chatty and articulate. If the Saturn finger is strong, she has an ability to concentrate on whatever she is doing.

A normal Mercury mount and a strong Saturn finger show a good brain.

OVERDEVELOPED

A large or puffy mount of Mercury denotes someone who is not always honest and reliable. This may be because she says what she thinks others want to hear; it does not necessarily mean that she is dishonest. However, if a large mount of Mercury is coupled with a crooked Mercury finger and a poor head line, she is less than trustworthy.

A poor Mercury mount and a crooked little finger show someone who is easily swayed by other people.

THIN AND FLAT

A mount of Mercury that is thin and underdeveloped indicates someone with poor communication skills. She struggles to express herself, but you will not know why until you have explored the rest of her hand. A strong head line will help to compensate for a poor mount of Mercury, but a weak head line coupled with a thin mount of Mercury shows an inability to think things through and express ideas.

Expert tip

If the mount of Mercury has joined with the mount of Apollo, it shows someone who has a good turn of phrase, enjoys expressing herself and may even make a career out of it.

THE OUTER MOUNT OF MARS

WHERE   The fleshy pad between the mount of Mercury and the mount of the Moon

INDICATES   Moral courage

There are two mounts of Mars on the hand. The outer mount of Mars is found on the outer edge of the palm, below the mount of Mercury and above the mount of the Moon, and indicates moral courage.

In astrology, Mars is the planet of energy, stamina, courage and aggression. It also indicates the level and nature of our drive and motivation.

NORMAL

Someone with a firm and well-developed outer mount of Mars has integrity and is honest. However, you should always check the Mercury mount and finger, because these may tell a different story. You will then have to look at the head line for further information.

OVERDEVELOPED

A very large outer mount of Mars indicates someone who holds very strong beliefs and convictions, to the point of exaggeration and dogmatism. This person may pride himself on his moral code and, if other factors in the

When the outer mount of Mars is very large, the person is unwavering in his beliefs. He will defend his ideas at all costs.

hand support it, may go to almost any lengths in order to follow his code.

For instance, he could be the dogged campaigner who refuses to give up the fight, even when he is clearly losing, because he believes it is the right thing to do and that his cause is just.

THIN AND FLAT

An outer mount of Mars that is very flat and flabby to the touch shows someone who finds it difficult to stick to his beliefs and who will soon cave in to the opposition. He is easily cowed by those who are more forceful than him.

THE INNER MOUNT OF MARS

WHERE The fleshy pad between the mount of Jupiter and the mount of Venus

INDICATES Physical courage

The inner mount of Mars sits on the inner edge of the palm, between the mount of Jupiter and the mount of Venus, and indicates physical courage.

NORMAL

A well-developed inner mount of Mars denotes someone who is courageous and prepared to fight for what he believes in—sometimes literally, if he thinks the cause is justified. He may have chosen a career in the armed services, or be an active campaigner for an issue about which he feels strongly.

OVERDEVELOPED

A very large and fleshy inner mount of Mars indicates someone who has so much energy and courage that he is likely to rush into dangerous situations without thinking. He may wade into a fight in the street and try to separate the warring sides, with no thought for his own safety. But his impulsiveness and foolhardiness may make the situation worse, and even put him at risk. A strong head line will help to counteract these reckless tendencies but a weak one will make them worse.

The combination of a very small or flat inner mount of Mars and a thick thumb indicates someone who is afraid of life and who copes by being belligerent.

THIN AND FLAT

When this mount is so underdeveloped that it is barely present on the hand, it indicates someone who has little physical courage. This may mean that he avoids trouble at all costs because he cannot cope with it, or it may make him overcompensate by being a bully, especially if he has a very thick thumb.

THE PLAIN OF MARS

WHERE The center of the palm

INDICATES Self-confidence

In astrology, Mars shows our ability to stand up for ourselves and reveals our level of confidence. It is a very energetic planet and takes its name from the Roman god of war.

NORMAL

A normal plain of Mars is springy and firm, and denotes someone who is self-assured and at ease when dealing with other people. She is not over-confident, but has a good sense of her own strengths and is able to cope in most situations.

OVERDEVELOPED

The thicker and more resilient the plain of Mars, the more confident the person. A very elastic and well-developed plain of Mars shows natural self-assurance and ebullience. If the plain is very hard and full, she is so sure of herself that she has a tendency to be bumptious and unfeeling. She may seem to ignore other people's emotions or dismiss them as silly, and she will push her way through life with little thought for the impact she is having on others.

UNDERDEVELOPED

If you can feel the bones and muscles beneath the skin in the center of the palm, the plain of Mars is underdeveloped. This means that the person in question is shy and lacks confidence, even though she may have

Expert tip

Unlike the other mounts on the hand, you can only assess the plain of Mars by touching it. The best way to do this is to run the ball of your thumb gently over the area while the other person's hand is extended but relaxed.

learned to cover this up well. Check the Jupiter mount and finger to find out if these are strong and will therefore help to compensate for her shyness by giving her an outward show of composure and ease.

The plain of Mars is situated in the center of the palm. Its exact shape will vary from hand to hand.

THE MOUNT OF VENUS

WHERE The pad enclosed by the life line that curls around it; although it is called a mount, it is in fact the pad of flesh that covers the base of the thumb

INDICATES The ability to express emotion and affection, as well as the general level of vitality

In astrology, Venus is the planet of love, describing how we show affection to ourselves and others. It is also the planet of beauty and social skills.

NORMAL

A springy, well-rounded mount of Venus indicates good physical stamina and plenty of energy. This person is sociable and outgoing, friendly and easy to get along with. He may also have artistic abilities that he uses in his career. He is convivial and outgoing, and his relationships are usually happy and successful.

OVERDEVELOPED

Someone with a very high, overdeveloped mount of Venus has a strong sex drive. It may be so powerful that it sometimes gets him into trouble. He rushes headlong into life and has so much energy that he is still going strong when everyone around him has collapsed in a heap from exhaustion.

FLAT AND FLABBY

A very flat or flabby mount of Venus shows a lack of energy and libido. The person in question may have problems with his health, especially if his life line is poor, and will struggle to have satisfying relationships because of difficulties in expressing his feelings and connecting wholeheartedly with others. Examine the heart line before reaching any definite conclusions, because this may compensate for an underdeveloped mount of Venus, although it will not make up for it entirely.

Expert tip

The mount of Venus also describes musical ability (or lack of it). A very angular joint where the base of the thumb joins the wrist (known as the "angle of rhythm") shows a good sense of rhythm. If the middle phalange of the thumb ends in a very angular joint, the person has a good sense of timing (this joint being known as the "angle of timing").

THE MOUNT OF THE MOON

WHERE The fleshy pad on the outer edge of the palm, running from below the outer mount of Mars to the wrist

INDICATES Sensitivity, imagination and intuition

Astrologers believe that the Moon represents our unconscious minds, intuition and the way we react to our surroundings.

NORMAL

A mount of the Moon that is firm but not too prominent indicates someone who has a good imagination and an equally strong artistic sense. Her intuition works well, and she may have a creative talent that she enjoys using. She is compassionate toward others and likes to create harmony.

OVERDEVELOPED

If this mount is extremely large, she is very imaginative, sometimes to the point of confusing fantasy and reality. She can talk herself into believing whatever she wants to believe, especially if her head line is weak.

THIN AND FLAT

A flat mount of the Moon denotes someone who is a complete realist. She thinks that seeing is believing, and has little or no imagination. If you are reading her palm, it is probably because she wants to disprove everything you tell her.

A LOW MOUNT

Look to see where the mount ends, because sometimes it stops well below the mount of Venus. This is most commonly seen on a water hand, where it shows that the person is extremely sensitive, not just emotionally, but also to atmospheres and her surroundings. A low mount of the Moon on an air hand indicates someone who finds it easy to express her strong imagination. On an earth hand, it represents someone with good creative skills and the imagination to put them into practice. On a fire hand, her imagination can sometimes run away with her, so she is not always a reliable source of information because it is so easy for her to embroider the facts unwittingly.

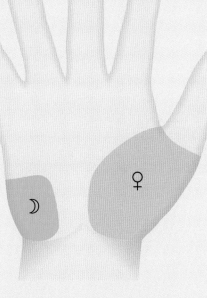

Always check to see whether the mount of the Moon ends below the mount of Venus, as it does here.

PERCUSSION

WHERE The outer edge of the palm

INDICATES Creative imagination

"Percussion" is the name that palmists give to the curve on the outer edge of the palm. In some hands this is very apparent, while in others the palm is virtually straight.

CURVED

The more pronounced the curve, the more pronounced that person's creative energy. A curve that is very noticeable shows someone whose creativity is not confined to artistic activities, but who enjoys many different forms of self-expression. For instance, he may love baking or cultivating a thriving

vegetable garden (both of which are creative activities in the widest sense), as well as having other artistic interests, such as painting pictures or playing a musical instrument.

STRAIGHT

If there is no curve, and the edge of the hand seems completely straight, that person has little or no creative imagination and instead takes a very rational approach to life. His home may be rather drab and functional, because he is simply not interested in making it look any different. As

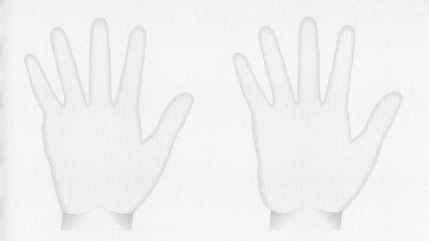

A high curve near the Mercury finger shows someone with plenty of ideas.

A low curve near the wrist shows someone with good, practical ideas.

far as he is concerned, he has more important things to do than fuss around choosing curtains or examining paint charts.

THE POSITION OF THE CURVE

Where exactly is the curve on the edge of the palm? Its position will give you important information about the nature of the person's creative energy.

A curve that is greatest at the top of the palm, near the mount of Mercury, shows someone who is full of ideas, but who may not necessarily put them into action. When the curve is fullest in the middle, the person has strong creative ideas and is able to see them through to completion. If the curve is strongest at the base of the palm, his ideas have a practical quality and stand a good chance of being feasible.

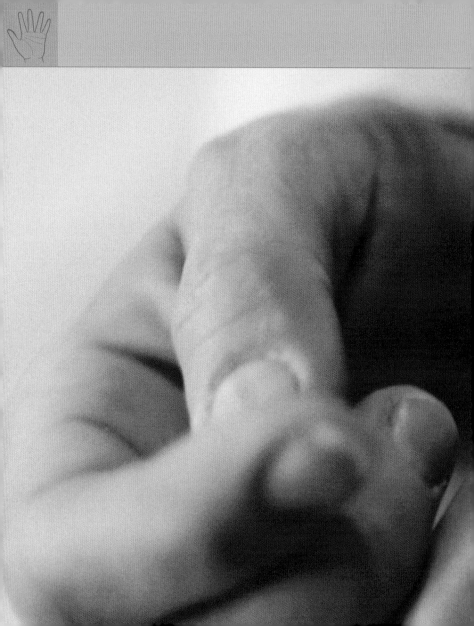

THE FINGERS
AND THUMBS

Until you start to examine plenty of hands, you may imagine that most people's fingers and thumbs look fairly similar, in which case you will be in for quite a shock.

In fact, fingers and thumbs can differ dramatically from one person to the next. Some fingers look like fat sausages, padded with so much flesh that they are puffy. Other fingers are almost skeletal, with the joints standing out in relief and the skin clinging to the bones. Of course, you will find people who are thin and have equally thin fingers, and those who are overweight with fat fingers, but this is not an unbreakable rule and you will come across slim people with fat fingers, and vice versa. It is always especially interesting to look at hands that do not match the person's physical build, so the hands therefore have a great deal to tell you.

WHAT THE FINGERS AND THUMBS SAY

You have now reached the stage when you must examine someone's fingers and thumbs in close detail. They will give you plenty of information about that person. Do not forget to look at both hands, because very often there will be slight variations in the shape or thickness of the fingers and thumbs of the left and right hands. Sometimes you will even find that a finger or thumb on one hand is shorter than that on the other.

LONG AND SHORT FINGERS

Not all fingers are of comparable length. Some are extra-long, as though they have been stretched like elastic; others are short and stubby. You can find a mixture of long and short fingers on one hand, too. All these shapes tell their own story, as you will discover in the coming pages, adding to the information you have already gathered from examining the basic shape of the hand.

THE USUAL LENGTH OF THE FINGERS

1 *Middle (Saturn) finger—longest*
2 *Index (Jupiter) finger*
3 *Ring (Apollo) finger*
4 *Little finger (Mercury)—shortest*

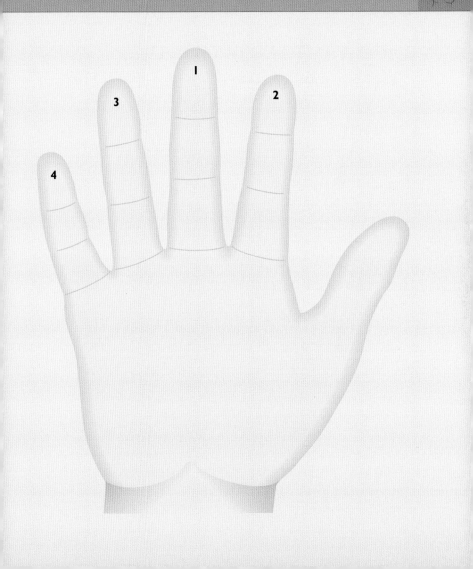

There is a strong curve where the base of the fingers meets the palm on this hand. This means the fingers cannot be measured by eye because their apparent lengths will be misleading.

MEASURING THE FINGERS

One of the techniques you need to master is measuring one finger against the next. When doing this, you must always check that the fingers are level at the base, because the top of the palm in some hands has a strong curve, so the little or Mercury finger may start much lower down the palm than the ring or Apollo finger. What at first glance looks like a very short Mercury finger may therefore turn out to be of average length, or sometimes even longer than average.

To measure the fingers, gently cup the palm until the bases of all the fingers are level. Ensure that the fingers are held straight, not curved, so that you can compare their lengths.

Usually the middle or Saturn finger is the longest, followed by the index or Jupiter finger, which should stop halfway up the middle of the top phalange of the Saturn finger. If the Jupiter finger ends below this point, it is considered short; if it ends beyond this point, it is long. The Apollo finger also normally stops halfway up the middle of the top phalange of the Saturn finger, but below the Jupiter finger. The Mercury finger is considered long if it extends beyond the start of the top phalange of the Apollo finger. It is very short if it ends below the top phalange.

In order to measure the fingers against one another when the top of the palm is very curved, the hand should be cupped so the fingers are all level at the point where they join the palm.

LOOKING AT THE THUMBS

Pay plenty of attention to the shape and size of the thumbs. Thumbs tell you a great deal about someone's will and energy, intellect and strength of character. Once you become accustomed to looking at hands, you will probably always instinctively glance at the thumbs of the people you meet, even if you are not giving them a reading, purely because their thumbs will tell you so much about them. For instance, someone may adopt behavioral strategies to disguise her terrible temper, but one glance at her thick, bulbous thumb will reveal her true character to you.

RINGS

The number of rings that someone wears, and the fingers or thumbs she wears them on, also tell a story. Fashion plays a part in this, of course, because rings for thumbs and index fingers have become popular again in recent years. Even so, the person who wears a ring on one of her fingers or thumbs is giving you important information about herself, because rings always strengthen the characteristics of the finger or thumb on which they are worn. So someone who wears a large ring on a weak Jupiter finger wants to bolster her ego and leadership abilities.

You should also note the sort of ring the person is wearing. Is it ostentatious or discreet? Antique or contemporary? Such information will help you build up a picture of the person whose palms you are reading.

Expert tip
Practice noticing the shapes of fingers and thumbs by looking at the hands of people you meet or those of people you see on television.

THE SHAPES OF THE FINGERS

Look at the end of each finger, because that will give you added information about someone's character and personality. At this point you are still building up a picture of the person's psychological make-up, whether by confirming characteristics you have already noticed elsewhere on the hand or by discovering traits you have not seen suggested anywhere else on the hand.

THE FOUR FINGER SHAPES

Each finger ends in one of four shapes: spatulate, square, pointed or conic. However, as you will discover when you start to look at lots of hands, it is unusual to find a hand in which every finger ends in the same shape, because most hands feature a mixture of two different shapes.

You can understand what the shape of each finger means simply by combining the meaning of the finger shape (such as spatulate) with the meaning of the finger itself (such as the Jupiter finger). For example, a spatulate Jupiter finger shows someone who is inventive (spatulate) and confident about showing it (Jupiter finger). If the majority of fingers conform to a particular shape, that is the dominant shape of the hand and it will have more impact on the person's character than the other finger shapes.

If each finger is a different shape, the person has a complex and changeable personality that is difficult to define. If this is the case, the shape of their hand will be helpful, as it will show their basic character.

A spatulate finger widens just before the tip.

A square finger is flat and squared off at the tip.

Spatulate

A spatulate finger widens toward the tip, almost as though the finger were being splayed out by being pressed against a hard surface. It has a more exaggerated shape than a square finger, and with a little practice you will soon notice the difference. A spatulate finger indicates someone who is energetic, original and innovative. For instance, he may be very sporty and always wants to be active. He may even try to persuade you to stop reading his palm and go for a swim with him instead.

Square

A square finger is level at the top and denotes someone who is conventional, practical and organized. He has a strong grasp of reality, which is increased according to the number of square fingers on the hand. If he has mostly square fingers combined with an earth hand, your only chance of reading his palm may come from observation, because he will tell you stoutly that he does not believe in such things as palmistry.

A pointed finger has a noticeably pointed tip.

A conic finger is gently rounded at the tip.

Pointed

A pointed finger shows someone who is highly creative and usually lives in a world of his own. He is very sensitive and easily hurt, so it can be difficult for him to cope with harsh realities. The more pointed fingers there are on the hand, the more dreamy and idealistic that person is—he is someone who likes to daydream (especially if he has water hands). You may wonder how he manages to get through life because he seems so unworldly and innocent.

Conic

A conic finger has a rounded tip. This is a less pronounced shape than a pointed finger, which is how you are able to see the difference between them. Someone with a conic finger is impulsive, impressionable and changeable. He has strong instincts that guide him through life—whether these instincts are helpful or otherwise. He acts on his hunches, so he may enjoy placing bets on horses because he is convinced they will win, or he may tell you that he has a gut feeling about something.

THE PHALANGES AND PADS

Now it is time to look at the sections of the fingers, which are known as "phalanges." The section nearest the palm is called the base phalange, the central section is the middle phalange, and the top third of the finger is the top phalange.

You need to look at the quality and shape of the three phalanges, as well as the differences between them. Is one phalange much longer than the other two? Is one noticeably shorter or thicker than the other two? You can judge this by eye, or by measuring the phalanges with your own fingers. To do this, hold the finger of one hand against the same finger on the other hand and judge the phalanges accordingly (for instance, check the top phalange of your right Jupiter finger against each phalange in turn of your left Jupiter finger). However, when measuring the base phalange, make sure that you measure it from the top of the knuckle joint.

THE PHALANGES
1 *Top phalange*
2 *Middle phalange*
3 *Bottom phalange*

Phalange characteristics

Finger	Phalange	Length	Meaning
Jupiter (Index)	Base	Short	Common-sensical
		Long	Bossy
	Middle	Short	Lacking drive
		Long	Ambitious
	Top	Short	Intuitive
		Long	Opinionated
Saturn (Middle)	Base	Short	Self-serving
		Long	Materialistic
	Middle	Short	Impractical
		Long	Practical
	Top	Short	Impetuous
		Long	Good at reasoning
Apollo (Ring)	Base	Short	Lacking artistic interest
		Long	Acquisitive
	Middle	Short	Clever with hands
		Long	Mentally adept
	Top	Short	Dreamy
		Long	Able to turn ideas into reality
Mercury (Little)	Base	Short	Lacking imagination
		Long	Chatty
	Middle	Short	Communicative
		Long	Reliable
	Top	Short	Having a retentive mind
		Long	Quick-thinking

CHECKING FOR THICKNESS

You must also examine the thickness of the phalanges. Some fingers have very thin middle phalanges, giving them what is known as a "waisted" appearance. Others have very thin base phalanges, although the middle and top phalanges are thick. A good way to discover the thickness of the phalanges is to hold the hand flat with the fingers together, and then to look at them against a light background. Any large gaps between the fingers will immediately be noticeable, highlighting thin phalanges.

THICK BASE PHALANGES

If the base phalanges are very thick, with no gaps between them, the person has a sensual approach to life. She likes material comforts and sets great store by her acquisitions. She also has a tendency to put herself first. If other indications on the hand confirm it, this may be someone who believes that she is what she owns and who is materialistic.

THIN BASE PHALANGES

If the base phalanges are so thin that there are gaps between them, the person is open and friendly, and generous with her money and affections. The wider the gaps, the more difficult it may be for her to keep hold of her money, although this

The phalanges on this hand are considerably thicker at the base.

may be because she tends to give it away, rather than because she spends it on herself. She will tend to put others' needs before her own.

LOOKING AT THE DROPLETS

It is also important to examine the pads, which are known as "droplets," on the backs of the top phalanges of the fingers. These are soft, raised patches of skin and one of the best ways to see them is when the hand is held out flat, with the palm down and the fingers pointing downward. The droplets will then stand out in relief. Not every hand has them, but when they are present they show that the person is very sensitive toward her surroundings, possibly to the point of being psychic. She also has strong artistic talents and appreciation. If the backs of the top phalanges are firm, with no droplets, she is very realistic and matter-of-fact about life, and has good business abilities.

This hand has base phalanges that are much thinner than the other two.

Droplets are small, soft pads of skin on the backs of the top phalanges.

THE JOINTS AND NAILS

Two of the most telling areas of someone's hands are the joints and nails on the fingers. You will want to examine them when you are reading someone's palm, but you can also take a look at them if you are meeting someone for social or business reasons and want to establish what sort of person you are dealing with. Casually glance at their fingers without staring.

Smooth finger joints like these show someone who acts intuitively.

Knotty finger joints like these show someone who thinks things through.

JOINTS

Look at the joints connecting the base and middle phalanges, and those connecting the middle and top phalanges of the fingers. Are they smooth and flat, or knotty and prominent? Are they all one type?

Smooth

If someone's fingers are very smooth and the joints are barely noticeable, he relies on his instincts, intuition and gut feelings when making decisions. He reaches conclusions based on how he feels about a situation, and this applies whether he is dealing with business or his private life. If his fingers are very short, he is extremely impulsive and probably rushes into situations without thinking them through carefully. Long fingers help to counteract the impulsive nature of smooth joints, so this person is more likely to look before leaping, although he may not always do so.

Knotty

When someone's joints are very bumpy and noticeable, it means that he thinks carefully before taking action. This may make him seem slow and deliberate, but his mind is working ceaselessly, analyzing the pros and cons of a situation, evaluating his position and recalling similar circumstances from the past. Short fingers and knotty joints mean that he sometimes acts on an impulsive streak, whereas long fingers and knotty joints indicate someone who will mull over problems for ages before doing anything about them.

NAILS

Nails are a mine of information once you know what to look for, and you will spend many happy hours studying people's nails so that you can find out what they are really like. Watch a politician on television and decide whether the political message matches

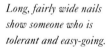

*Long, fairly wide nails
show someone who is
tolerant and easy-going.*

*Short nails with a gap
between the nail and
fingertip show petulance.*

*Short, wide nails show a
critical and rather
intolerant nature.*

what the nails are saying. Sometimes you will be very surprised indeed by what you find.

Length

The first thing to check is whether the nails are long or short. A normal-sized nail is half the length of the top phalange of a finger or thumb. If the nails are longer than this, the person lives in his imagination and rarely comes down to earth or faces up to reality. If the nails are shorter than usual, he is logical, argumentative and critical of people who do not behave in the way he expects or wants.

Width

How wide are the nails? If they are very narrow, the person is narrow-minded and reluctant to accept any point of view that does not agree with his own. It will take a lot of convincing before he changes his mind about something, and you may go blue in the face trying. The wider the nails, the

Long, narrow nails reveal narrow-mindedness and a reluctance to take risks.

more patient and open-minded someone is, with a tendency to be more honest than tactful—sometimes with unfortunate results. However, nails that are wide and short indicate someone who is opinionated and critical of others.

Other features

If there is a noticeable gap between the top of someone's nail and his fingertip, he has an explosive temper, although his outbursts never last long.

Expert tip

Are the half-moons visible at the base of the nails? Visible moons are a sign of good health, unless they are very large, in which case they can indicate health problems. Very pale or absent moons indicate someone whose health may be affected by circumstances, such as always getting colds when feeling under pressure.

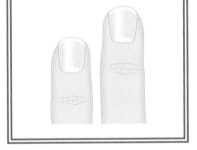

Check to see if he bites or tears his nails, as this means he is nervy and is dealing with a situation in which he feels out of his depth.

GETTING TO KNOW THE FINGERS

It helps to become familiar with as many palmistry terms as possible. You will then find it easier to read and understand this book, and you will be able to call the parts of the hand by their proper names when talking about them to other palmists. You can also use these palmistry terms when you are reading someone's hand, provided that you explain what you are talking about to the other person. Gradually building up your knowledge of palmistry will help you remember it more easily than trying to cram all the information into your head in one session. If you find it difficult to remember the correct palmistry terms for the fingers, try to invent a rhyme or other memorable device. For instance, you could make up a saying that uses the letters J, S, A and M in that order, to help you remember that the names of the fingers are Jupiter, Saturn, Apollo and Mercury.

THE NAMES
OF THE FINGERS
1 *Saturn finger*
2 *Jupiter finger*
3 *Apollo finger*
4 *Mercury finger*
5 *Thumb*

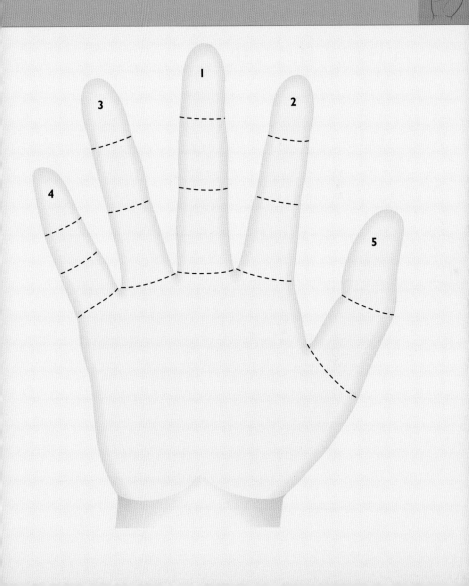

THE THUMB

INDICATES   Character, willpower, logic, temper

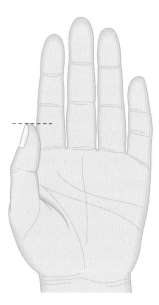

NORMAL

A normal thumb is more or less the same length as the little or Mercury finger. When the thumb is held against the side of the hand, it should reach halfway up the base phalange of the index or Jupiter finger. This indicates someone with a well-balanced ego, who can assert herself when necessary, but is not a bully, and who has a healthy amount of motivation and drive.

Measure the thumb against the base phalange of the Jupiter finger.

A short thumb and bulbous top phalange indicate a bad temper.

LONG

A thumb that ends past the middle of the base phalange of the Jupiter finger is long, indicating that this person is good at managing other people and likes taking charge of situations. Watch out if the thumb is really long, because this is someone who can be overbearing, domineering and convinced that she is always right. She is a bully.

SHORT

Someone's thumb is short if it fails to reach the middle of the Jupiter finger's base phalange. This person prefers others to take charge and likes to drift along in their wake, being looked after and told what to do. She will be out of her depth if placed in a position of leadership. If you meet her socially, she will be happy for you to make all the arrangements.

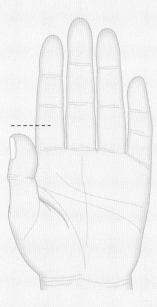

TOP PHALANGE

The thumb is divided into two sections: the top and middle phalanges. Just as you did with the fingers, you need to examine the length of the phalanges to see if one is longer than the other. It may help to use a ruler to do this, because some thumbs are quite deceptive.

The top phalange rules will power: if it is long, it denotes someone who knows what she wants and likes to get her own way as much as possible. Now check the thickness of this phalange. The thicker it is from front to back, the more outspoken that person is and the more determined to have things all her own way. This is especially true if the back of the phalange is bulbous, in which case she has quite a temper. Be wary of someone who has a weak thumb with a very fat top phalange, because it can indicate violent tendencies. She can only get her own way through bullying. Someone with a flat or thin top phalange is nervy and highly sensitive to the atmosphere around her.

MIDDLE PHALANGE

The middle phalange rules logic, so if it is longer than the top phalange this shows someone who likes to mull over decisions at her leisure. The tendency

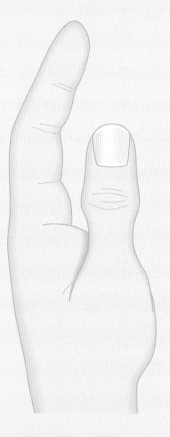

The middle phalange of this thumb is narrow ("waisted"). It indicates good diplomatic skills.

is increased if she has knotty finger joints. How wide is the middle phalange? If it is narrow at the center (which palmists call "waisted"), it shows someone who is tactful and charming. She knows how to handle other people to get the best out of them. If this phalange is very narrow, she loves analyzing situations and has a horror of rushing into decisions.

POSITION

Look to see where the thumb starts on the hand. The normal position is midway down the hand, in which case the person has an average ego and practical ability.

If the thumb starts high on the hand, near the Jupiter finger, she has a strong ego and equally strong opinions, which she will be very keen to share with you. If the thumb starts low on the hand, near the wrist, she has a powerful practical streak, but not much imagination. Sometimes a low thumb can indicate a low level of intellect. The head line will tell you more.

RINGS

If someone wears a ring on one of her thumbs, it shows that she wants to bolster her ego and will power. Is this to compensate for weak thumbs (in which case she may well need extra confidence) or does the ring accentuate what are already strong thumbs (in which case she is a force to be reckoned with and will always want to get her own way)?

Expert tip

Check the length of the Mercury finger before measuring the thumb against it. If the finger is long, so is the thumb.

THE JUPITER FINGER

WHERE The index finger

INDICATES Self-confidence, pride, ego

NORMAL

How long is the finger? A normal Jupiter finger reaches halfway up the top phalange of the Saturn finger and shows that the person has a good level of self-confidence without being arrogant and domineering. He takes a reasonable, healthy pride in his achievements without feeling the need to brag about them to all and sundry.

LONG

A Jupiter finger that reaches more than halfway up the top section of the Saturn finger is considered long, signifying that the person has strong ambitions and a highly developed sense of his own power. He may be egocentric and arrogant, as though no one else in the world exists but him. He is certainly confident, but does he use that confidence wisely or throw his weight around? The quality and shape of his thumbs will tell you more about this, because they will reveal whether he is able to channel his energies in a positive direction (as shown by a thumb of normal length) or is full of ideas that never come to anything (as shown by a weak, thin thumb).

SHORT

A short Jupiter finger denotes someone who is shy and slightly withdrawn. He prefers to be told what to do rather than take the lead of his own accord. He makes an excellent helper or assistant because his ego does not need to be bolstered by having power and control over others. However, if his thumb is weak as well, he may try to avoid taking responsibility whenever possible, because he does not feel able to cope with it.

RINGS

Does this person wear a ring on either of his Jupiter fingers? If so, which hand has he chosen and how big is the ring? Wearing a ring on one finger unconsciously emphasizes the meaning of that finger, so a ring on the Jupiter finger means that he wants to boost his self-confidence and sense of personal power. Someone who wears a ring on his weak Jupiter finger therefore wants to feel more capable and self-assured. If you meet someone wearing a ring on a long Jupiter finger, you will soon discover that he is very sure of himself

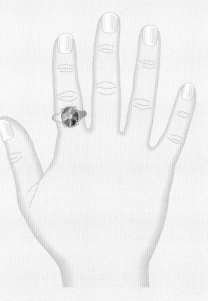

A flashy ring on a short Jupiter finger indicates someone who wants to increase his confidence and ego.

and of his place in the world; invariably he thinks you come a poor second to him. The bigger the ring, the greater his need to assert his ego.

Someone wearing a ring on the Jupiter finger of his dominant hand wants to take action and be noticed through his achievements. If he wears the ring on his nondominant hand, it means that he would like to be more assertive but for some reason is unable to achieve this.

GAPS BETWEEN THE FINGERS

Ask the person to hold his fingers together so that you can see whether there is a gap between the Jupiter and Saturn fingers. If there is, he is good at managing his time and abilities, so this is a promising sign if you are interviewing him for a job or hoping to work with him as a colleague.

Does the finger look as though it is part of the hand, or as though it was stuck on as an afterthought? A finger that seems to stand apart from the rest of the hand indicates someone who loves being in the spotlight, especially if the finger is long and/or adorned with a ring. This person always wants to be the center of attention, which may be amusing for a while but can mean that ultimately he wants everyone else to be an appreciative audience that never interrupts him.

Expert tip

Does the Jupiter finger lean toward the Saturn finger? If so, it denotes someone who likes to acquire possessions, perhaps to give him a stronger sense of security. He also has a cautious approach to life.

A gap between the Jupiter and Saturn
fingers shows someone who is in control.

When the Jupiter finger stands apart, the
person likes being in the limelight.

THE SATURN FINGER

WHERE The middle finger

INDICATES Responsibility, authority, conscientiousness

NORMAL

The Saturn finger is usually the longest finger on the hand, rising above its neighboring Jupiter and Apollo fingers. However, these fingers may be very long or very short, so a good way to find the length of the Saturn finger is to measure it against the palm: an average Saturn finger is three-quarters the length of the palm.

A normal Saturn finger shows someone who has a good sense of responsibility without letting it rule her life or turn her into a martyr. She works hard but knows when to stop.

LONG

Someone with a long Saturn finger has an overdeveloped sense of responsibility. She might volunteer for more than her fair share of work because she feels it is expected of her, even though that may not be the case at all. She is dependable and trustworthy and excels in business, but finds it hard to relax because she is acutely aware of all the things she thinks she should be doing. If this person is a guest at a party, you will probably find her offering to hand round the food or in the kitchen.

The Saturn finger looks shorter than it really is because the Apollo finger is longer than normal.

SHORT

Someone with a short Saturn finger has a horror of being given any sort of responsibility; she would much rather someone else did all the work. Look at the rest of her hand for clues about why this should be, such as laziness or a lack of confidence. The shorter her Saturn finger, the less able she is to make decisions and commitments. For instance, she may prefer to remain single rather than have to choose whom to marry, or she may drift through life letting others make every important decision for her.

HEAVY

A Saturn finger that looks much heavier and thicker than the other fingers belongs to someone who has a tendency to make a major drama out of her problems. She regards difficulties as insurmountable crises, rather than as challenges that can be overcome, and quickly becomes discouraged by them.

This very long Saturn finger is further emphasized by a signet ring.

RINGS

Is this person wearing any rings on either of her Saturn fingers? If so, she unconsciously wants to increase her sense of security and her feeling of being important in the world. Often this is because the world feels like an unsafe place to her, perhaps because

of a childhood trauma such as her parents getting divorced. Someone with a ring on a short Saturn finger is trying to compensate for her reluctance to accept responsibility. If someone wears a ring on her long Saturn finger, she rarely sees her home and family because she is so busy working round the clock. The style of ring worn on this finger is also informative. A classic signet ring on a long Saturn finger shows someone who wants to look traditional and reliable. Appearances are important to her.

GAPS BETWEEN THE FINGERS

Look to see if there are any gaps between the Jupiter and Saturn, or Saturn and Apollo, fingers. A gap between the Jupiter and Saturn fingers shows someone who is a good manager and who can be depended on at work because she is strongly motivated. If there is a gap between the Saturn and Apollo fingers, she likes to live for the present and let the future take care of itself. She finds it very hard to save for a rainy day and is not good at forward planning.

Expert tip

Look to see whether the Saturn finger leans toward the Jupiter or Apollo finger. When it leans toward the Jupiter finger, it shows someone who would like to have more self-confidence; when it leans toward the Apollo finger, it indicates a desire to take life less seriously than she feels she has to, perhaps because of family commitments.

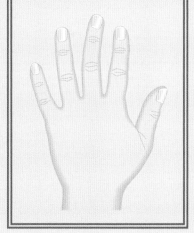

THE APOLLO FINGER

WHERE The ring finger

INDICATES Creativity, emotions, the ability to feel happy

NORMAL

A normal Apollo finger is slightly shorter than the Jupiter finger, which in turn is slightly shorter than the Saturn finger. It indicates someone who has a good artistic and creative sense and enjoys expressing it. He may not be overwhelmingly artistic, but neither is he useless at such things. He finds it easy to show his feelings and is sociable.

LONG

A long Apollo finger indicates someone who has strong emotions that he finds hard to hide. He may cry at the drop of a handkerchief, but is also easily amused. In other words, his feelings are always near the surface and ready to be expressed. He has a strong artistic flair, although you will have to look at the rest of the hand to see what form this takes: It might be an ability to draw, write, dance, sing or do gymnastics. He is good company and is often the sort of person that you feel better for knowing, because he has the happy knack of being able to cheer up anyone who feels miserable. He has life-enhancing qualities.

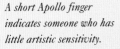

A short Apollo finger indicates someone who has little artistic sensitivity.

SHORT

A short Apollo finger indicates that someone does not have much interest in artistic matters and probably cannot see why anyone else would, either. He is not a philistine, but does not pay much attention to the look of his home or the style of his clothes, because he thinks such things are unimportant. As for emotions, he finds it difficult to express them, which can make it seem as though he is unfeeling and insensitive, even though this is not true. He may lack energy and drive, and has a tendency to be slightly pessimistic when things go wrong.

RINGS

Is the person wearing a ring on one of his Apollo fingers? The custom of wearing a wedding ring on the right or left hand varies from country to country, so you might want to check this with the person in question, if you think he is wearing his ring on the wrong hand. However, not everyone who is married wears a wedding ring. This is less unusual among men, but it can be quite striking if you meet a married woman who does not wear a ring. You may want to ask yourself why, and look for answers in her hand. Is it because she wants to retain some independence, or does she want to give the impression that she is still available? Is she making a feminist statement or is her marriage in trouble?

If a woman who is not in a long-term relationship is wearing what looks like an engagement or wedding ring on this finger, once again you should wonder why. Does it make her feel more secure? Is she repelling would-be suitors? Is she compensating for the lack of a partner? If in doubt, ask her, but choose your words carefully.

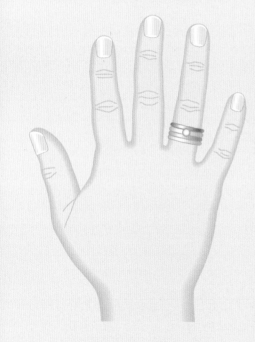

A long Apollo finger's impact increases when it is adorned by several rings.

Sometimes you will meet someone who has adorned both Apollo fingers with several rings. What does this say about him? The rest of his hand should tell you, but perhaps he feels emotionally insecure or wants to increase his creativity.

GAPS BETWEEN THE FINGERS

Is the Apollo finger separated from the Saturn or Mercury finger by a noticeable gap? A space between the Saturn and Apollo fingers indicates someone who lives for the moment and believes the future will take care of itself. A space between the Apollo and Mercury fingers indicates someone who is always slightly distanced from the rest of the world.

Expert tip

Does the Apollo finger lean toward one of its neighbors? If it leans toward the Saturn finger, it indicates someone who wishes he could be more responsible and fears that he does not take life seriously enough. If it leans toward the Mercury finger, he has a good flair for words and enjoys using them.

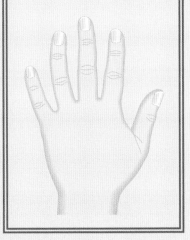

THE MERCURY FINGER

WHERE The little finger

INDICATES Communication abilities, honesty

NORMAL

Take care when measuring the length of the Mercury finger, because appearances can be deceptive. Sometimes this finger starts low down on the palm (which shows a lack of confidence), making it look much shorter than it really is. So make sure that the hand is cupped until the base of the Apollo and Mercury fingers are on the same level, before deciding on the length of the Mercury finger.

If the finger is a normal length, it reaches the start of the top phalange of the Apollo finger. This indicates someone who finds it easy to communicate with other people. However, her communication skills do not make her stand out in any way: She is neither too chatty nor too quiet.

LONG

Someone with a long Mercury finger has a great gift for communication. She is talkative, amusing and has an inventive turn of phrase that can be highly entertaining. She may make her living out of communicating with others, whether as a writer, teacher or broadcaster, or may simply be known

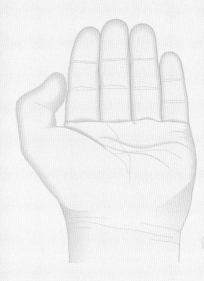

This Mercury finger is long because it reaches beyond the top phalange of the Apollo finger.

among her friends as someone who is great at telling stories and has a wonderful way with words.

Always check the Mercury fingers on both hands to see if they differ in some way. When one Mercury finger is longer or wider than the other, it has extra strength and becomes the most important of the two fingers. All the characteristics of that finger will be accentuated. If this is on the dominant

This Mercury finger is set low down on the hand but is surprisingly long.

hand, that person will consciously use those characteristics when communicating with others; if it is on the nondominant hand, she is not as aware of the way she communicates with others.

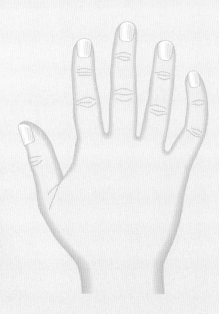

This long, curved Mercury finger shows a lively, if inaccurate, talker.

SHORT

Someone with a short Mercury finger struggles to put her thoughts and feelings into words. It is difficult for her to communicate with other people and she often gives the impression of being tongue-tied and lost for something to say. Next time you are in a social setting and someone is sitting quietly, not contributing much to the conversation, or has difficulty in getting her point across, check to see if this is because she has short Mercury fingers.

STRAIGHT OR CROOKED

As the Mercury finger rules communication, you need to check the honesty and accuracy of what is being said by looking to see whether the Mercury fingers are straight or crooked. A straight Mercury finger indicates straight talking, with that person abiding by the truth. However, a curved or bent Mercury finger suggests that she does not always stick to the truth. This may be because she embroiders her stories to make them more dramatic or interesting; because she tells little white lies; or because she is a complete crook. However, you must ignore fingers that have been damaged through illness or accident.

RINGS

Wearing a ring on the Mercury finger means that the person wants to demonstrate her sexual independence. If she is also wearing an engagement or wedding ring, this will give you some interesting information about her. If someone goes through a phase of wearing a ring on her Mercury finger and then takes it off, you might come to the conclusion that she has been going through an independent period in which she did not want to be tied down emotionally or sexually.

GAPS BETWEEN THE FINGERS

A gap between the Mercury and Apollo fingers denotes someone who is private and likes to keep a little part of herself closed off from the rest of the world. When it looks as though the Mercury finger is separate from the rest of the hand, she is very independent and will always keep her emotional distance from other people.

Expert tip

Does the Mercury finger lean toward the Apollo finger? If so, it shows someone who has an inventive way of talking. You will have to decide whether this means she invents the facts to suit herself or whether she has an original or fanciful turn of phrase.

THE LINES OF THE HAND

You might think that your hands are identical, but they are not. They may be the same shape, and the fingers may be of the same length, but once you start to study the lines on each palm you will realize how different your two hands are. You might even discover that your hands do not seem to match at all, almost as if they belong to two separate people. No wonder palmistry is so fascinating, because you never know what you will discover.

There is also a huge variation in the way the lines appear on people's palms. Some people have lines that are deeply etched into their palms, while others are so lightly drawn that you can see them only in a strong light. You may come across a hand covered in so many tiny lines that they resemble a cobweb stretching over the palm, or you might look at a hand that has only the major lines on it. This is all valuable information that you will be able to interpret with the help of this book.

WHAT THE LINES SAY

Why do we have lines on our palms? At first you might think the logical answer is that they are caused by creasing up our palms, and it is true that some of the lines do match the folds that are caused when we curl up our hands. But do all of them?

EXPLORING YOUR OWN HANDS

Take a good look at your own palms, curling and uncurling them while you watch what happens to the lines. Do all the lines match the way your hands fold up? Unless you only have the

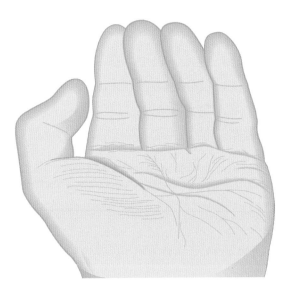

The dark creases on this palm are created when the hand is curled up. The other lines are not caused by the movement of the hand.

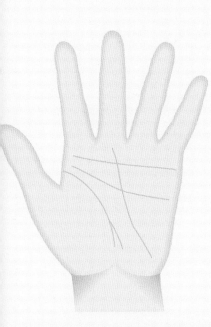

The fate, heart and head lines on this palm are clear but the life line is forked.

major lines on your palms, you will soon realize that some of the lines are not affected by any of the movements you make with your hands. This is especially true of some of the lines that appear on the mount of the Moon and the mount of Venus. They seem to be there quite independently of the way your hands move. Some of the small lines probably run together to create shapes and patterns that look like stars, crosses, boxes or little grills, often in places on your palm that are not affected by its movement. How can this be?

You will probably also notice that some of the major lines on your hand are strong and clear, whereas others are decorated with small lines that run across or beside them. Once again, these lines have no relation to the way your hand opens and closes, so why is there such variation in their quality? Other lines may have breaks in them, which seem to happen spontaneously or occur only on one hand, apparently having nothing to do with your hand's natural sequence of movements. All these strange anomalies can be answered by palmistry, as you are about to discover.

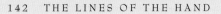

The energy of the fate line, running up the palm, is not as strong as that of the other lines.

LINES OF ENERGY

Each line on your palm describes the quality of the energy that is ruled by that line. The stronger the line, the more strongly its energy flows. And the weaker the line, or the more little lines that cut across it, the weaker that line's energy will be. This simple rule will help you when you start to read the lines and are confronted by their many diversities.

For instance, the heart line describes someone's ability to love himself and others, so when you see a faint or feathery heart line you will know that this person has emotional difficulties of some kind. You will have to look at his hand in more detail to find out exactly what has caused these problems, but one glance at the line will tell you that they exist. Conversely, a strong heart line shows someone who is very sure of his emotions and has no problems in expressing them.

However, this is not the end of the story with the heart line. A strong heart line, unaffected by little lines or marks, shows someone whose emotions are equally unaffected by other people or circumstances. He can therefore be rather self-centered and insensitive, because he remains impervious to the feelings of others.

READING THE LINES

The best way to start reading the lines is with your own hands. After all, you know yourself well, so you can apply the interpretations of the lines to your own life and personality. But you must be honest with yourself when you find characteristics in your hand that you are not proud of, and you must not be tempted to ignore or reinterpret them. If you lie to yourself about your character or gloss over unpleasant aspects, you will not learn much about palmistry and you will fail to discover much about yourself.

MISSING LINES

Each hand is unique. Some hands are covered with major and minor lines; others have only the major lines, as though they are interested in the essentials, but nothing else. And some hands have missing lines.

MISSING MAJOR LINES

It is very noticeable when one of the major lines is missing from someone's hand because it is so rare.

The first thing to do is to check that it really is missing and has not merged with another line, or that it is not so faint that you have mistaken it for a minor line. Head and heart lines that have merged together are called "simian lines" and are so important that they are dealt

with in more detail later in this section (see pages 214–215).

When you are sure that a line is missing, look and see if it is missing from both hands or just one, because this will tell you more about the significance of the line's absence. For

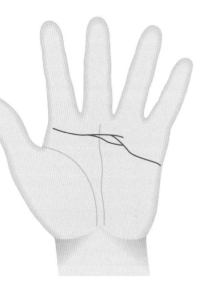

The heart and head lines have merged in this palm. The heart line is on the left and the head line on the right.

It is unusual but not impossible for a palm to be lacking the fate line, as shown in this example.

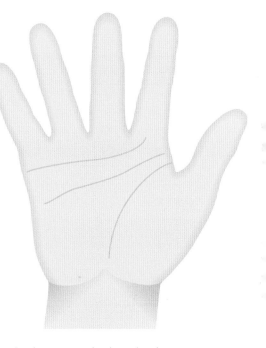

instance, if the person is left-handed and there is no fate line on her right hand, it shows that she works hard at achieving her ambitions and tends to live for today, rather than planning in advance. If she is left-handed and there is no fate line on that hand, she has a tendency to dream about what she is going to do, but rarely gets round to action. A fate line missing from both hands shows that the person in question likes to take each day as it comes and does not like being bogged down in a restrictive routine.

MISSING MINOR LINES

You are more likely to discover that some of the minor lines are missing from a hand. In each case you must note whether the line is present on the dominant or nondominant hand, because that will tell you whether the person is actively expressing the energies of the line (her dominant hand) or is doing so only in her imagination (her nondominant hand). Or is the line missing on both hands?

DOUBLE LINES

Now and then you will come across a hand with a double line—meaning that you will see the proper line accompanied by another line, which palmists call a "sister line," that runs beside it. Sometimes this sister line runs for the entire length of the main line; at other times it is visible only for a short stretch of the main line.

IS IT REALLY DOUBLE?

Before you decide that you have found a double line on someone's palm, you must check that you have not mistaken it for another line that is meant to be there. For instance, when looking at what you think is a double life line, you must make sure you are not looking at an ordinary life line accompanied by the line of Mars, which is a minor line that runs down the mount of Venus between the thumb and the life line.

Double lines usually sit very close to the main line, which is one good way of telling them apart from other minor lines.

LUCKY LINES

Double lines are traditionally considered to be very lucky, because they reinforce the energy of the line in question. A classic example is a double life line, which is believed to show a guardian angel is watching over that person. A double heart line shows that someone has an enormous amount of emotional energy, and his emotional life is bound to be important to him.

Double lines offer a form of protection to the main line. When you look carefully you will often notice that the second line appears just before the main line is damaged in some way. It might have a big or small break, or a line running at right angles to it, or some other marking that indicates a time of stress in that person's life. The double line reinforces the strength of the main line, almost as though it were supporting it during a difficult period.

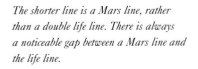

The shorter line is a Mars line, rather than a double life line. There is always a noticeable gap between a Mars line and the life line.

This is a classic example of a double life line. The sister line runs close to the life line for part of its length.

THE MAJOR LINES

For many people, interpreting the lines on someone's palm is one of the most exciting aspects of palmistry because no two hands are alike. It can seem rather challenging at first, because there are so many lines to learn and often many of these are affected by subsidiary lines or markings. Take time to build up your expertise so that you master the meaning of each line slowly.

The rest of this section is dedicated to the major and minor lines of the palm. Not every hand has every line, of course, but you need to know what each line looks like so that you can recognize it when you see it. This section also shows you where each line begins and ends, so that you will know which end of the line refers to childhood and which to the conclusion of the person's life.

THE FOUR
MAJOR LINES
a *Heart line*
b *Head line*
c *Life line*
d *Fate line*

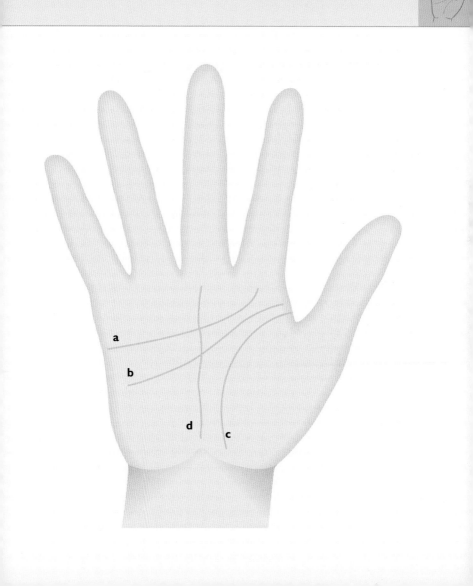

THE LIFE LINE

WHERE Between the thumb and the Jupiter finger

ENDS At the base of the mount of Venus

INDICATES The major events in a person's life

You can tell an enormous amount about someone from looking at her life line. It shows the milestones in her life and times of difficulty, but it also reveals the amount and quality of her physical energy. The beginning of the line describes her childhood and the end of the line indicates what will happen to her at the conclusion of her life.

THE START OF THE LINE

The life line begins at some point on the palm between the base of the Jupiter or index finger and the base of the thumb. Your first task is to find exactly where it starts, because that will tell you a lot about the person's character and her early life.

Normal

The average starting position for the life line is midway between the Jupiter finger and the base of the thumb. This shows someone who has a balanced attitude toward her ambitions, so she is not overwhelmingly determined to get ahead and not completely unmotivated, either. Her goals are important, but not compulsively so.

High

If the life line begins near or on the mount of Jupiter, that person is extremely ambitious and has known what she wants to do with her life from an early age. She has a lot of energy, although she may not always channel it in a physical direction and may have many intellectual interests.

POSSIBLE STARTING POINTS

a *Starts on or near the mount of Jupiter*
b *Starts midway between the index finger and the base of the thumb*
c *Starts close to the base of the thumb*

Low

If the life line begins close to the base of the thumb, the person does not have much ambition. She is very practical, and on the whole is much keener on physical activities than on mental pursuits.

The quality of the line

Look closely at the start of the line to check its strength. Is it strongly marked, feathery and fragile, or does it have small lines running across it? The quality of the line will reveal the quality of the person's childhood and early upbringing.

A strong and clearly marked line, without any small lines running across it or interfering with its energy in any way, indicates an easy-going childhood that was not interrupted by any major crises.

A feathery start to the life line shows that the childhood was difficult, perhaps with circumstances that confused the child or made her feel inadequate. Look to see whether the life lines on both hands start in the same way. If so, these childhood scars go much deeper than if only one hand is affected.

If there are many small lines crossing the start of the life line, that person's childhood was affected by numerous people. They may have interfered in the child's welfare or presented lots of obstacles for her to surmount. Other markings that might affect the start of the life line, such as crosses, stars and grills, are described later in this section (see pages 234–237).

Always be tactful when mentioning incidents that you suspect might be painful for the person concerned. Do not make blunt statements, such as announcing that she must have had a very unhappy childhood. Instead, approach the subject gently and be ready to move

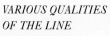

VARIOUS QUALITIES
OF THE LINE
a *Feathery*
b *Strong and clear*
c *Chained*
d *Bars crossing it*

This is a very weak life line because it is so feathery and it also has lines of interference running across it.

on to something else if she obviously does not want to discuss it.

Joined head and life lines

Sometimes the life line begins so high on the hand that it is joined to the start of the head line. When this happens, it indicates someone who lacks confidence when making decisions. She often knows her own mind, but for some reason feels she has to consult other people before reaching her final conclusion. This might be someone who has to refer every decision to her partner before making up her mind about it.

Fused head and heart lines can also indicate that someone had to cope with restrictions and setbacks at the start of her life. These might have been caused by difficult circumstances at home, such as lack of money or problems between her parents, or by attending a very strict school from an early age. You can use the timing techniques described later in this section (see pages 246–249) to find out how long the restrictions lasted.

Gap between the head and life lines

If the head and life lines begin separately, the size of the gap between the two of them will describe the person's level of independence. The bigger the gap, the more independent she is. So a very large gap between the start of the two lines suggests someone who is so determined to do her own thing that she is headstrong and possibly even foolish, because she will not listen to other people's advice.

THE END OF THE LINE

The next step is to see where and how the life line ends on the palm. This will give you some indication of how the person's life will end (although you must always bear in

POSSIBLE ENDING POINTS

a *Ends curved around the mount of Venus*

b *Ends with a fork pointing to the mount of the Moon*

mind that the formation of the lines can change, thereby altering her future) and will also give you information about her character. In most cases the line ends either curled around the base of the mount of Venus or forming a fork, with one branch pointing to the mount of the Moon and the other on the mount of Venus.

The end position

When the end of the life line is tucked around the mount of Venus, it shows someone who loves her home and looks on it as almost a sacred refuge from the rest of the world. If the life line forks and one branch of it runs out to the mount of the Moon, she enjoys traveling, but is equally happy to come home again. She is not good with a very strict routine, preferring a more spontaneous lifestyle in which she can be her own boss. However, she may be a born traveler if the fork running toward the mount of the Moon is stronger than the one heading toward the mount of Venus. If physical travel does not appeal, by the end of her life she will have traveled a long way from the circumstances at the beginning of her life.

The quality of the line

You need to examine the end of the life line to see how the person's life will conclude. Be very careful when discussing this and do not make any dire prognostications. You are simply looking to see whether the person's energy will fade away gradually or whether she will keep going strongly until she dies. If the line gets weaker as it ends, it shows that she will also get weaker as she nears the end of her life. If the end of the line is strong, she will be in good health until she dies. If the line becomes stronger as it nears its end, her life will become more dramatic, eventful and vital as she gets older.

a

b

*LIFE LINE FORKING
AT THE END*

a *Weaker line going down to the
base of the mount of Venus*

b *Stronger line forking to the
mount of the Moon*

A fork at the end of the line is a sign of good fortune and success. These are experienced during the life, rather than at the end of it. Remember that this person's idea of success may be very different from yours, but she will nevertheless achieve her ambitions and goals, whatever these are.

THE LENGTH OF THE LINE

Many people believe that a long life line equals a long life and therefore get very upset if their life line is short. Does this mean they will die early? Actually, it has no bearing on their life span at all, which should come as a relief to them. It is the *quality* of the line that is important, because a life line that is pale, thin or punctuated by breaks indicates someone who does not have much physical energy and vitality. A short life line that is strong, with few (if any) interruptions, indicates someone with a good level of energy, who therefore stands a good

chance of living to a ripe old age, despite the length of her life line.

THE CURVE OF THE LINE

Your next step is to assess the curve of the life line, because this is another indication of physical vitality, as well as revealing the person's enjoyment of life and her level of emotional generosity. Does the line swing out from its starting point in a nice wide sweep before curling back again, or does it hug the mount of Venus to such an extent that it looks almost straight as it runs down the palm?

Very curved

The bigger the curve of the line, the more generous, enthusiastic and lively the person is. It is almost as though her life line wants to get out into the world to experience as much as possible. This person is good company and has many interests. Always check both hands to see whether both lines have such a strong curve, or whether this is only present on one hand. If it is only on the dominant hand, she has overcome her innate emotional reservations and physical limitations to make the most of her life. If it is only present on the nondominant hand, she may feel frustrated by all the things she would like to do with her life, if only circumstances permitted it.

Slightly curved

When the line does not display a very generous curve, but is not completely straight, the person is rather reserved emotionally. She is shy and unsure of herself, and it may take time to get to know her properly. If you are meeting her for the first time, it may be difficult to get her to open up to you, especially if there is also a big gap between her Apollo and Mercury fingers. Look to see if she holds her thumbs close to her palms as well.

Straight

If the life line is almost straight, cutting through the mount of Venus rather than running around it, the person lacks emotional generosity, takes every opportunity to find fault with others and is really only interested in one person—herself. Describing this aspect of her character will test your powers of diplomacy to the limit, because no one wants to be on the receiving end of a character assassination.

THE REST OF THE LINE

Of course you must also pay attention to the rest of the line and not just to its beginning and end. Does it vary in strength or color? Are some areas free of small marks and others heavily affected by them? Does it flow in one continuous line from start to finish without any breaks (even minor ones), or is there a noticeable interruption in the line at some point?

WAYS THE LINE
CAN CURVE
a *Very curved*
b *Slightly curved*
c *Straight*

We will discuss the meaning of breaks in the line later on (see pages 240–245), but in the meantime there is still a lot to examine.

Variations in strength and color

If the line is sometimes pale and sometimes more defined, or the color varies along its length, you will know that this person's energy fluctuates during her life. The areas where the life line is strongly marked indicate the times when her energy will flow well. Equally, the areas where

The strength and quality of the life line are more important than its length. This line is short but very strong.

the life line is pale or gets thinner indicate the periods in her life when she is ill or hampered in some way. The techniques for timing events on the lines are described at the end of this section (see pages 246–249).

Look closely at these segments of life line to see if they are also affected by what palmists call "lines of interference," which are small horizontal lines that cross the main line and therefore block its flow of energy. The presence of these lines in a section of the life line that is also lacking in color or definition shows that the person is going through a really hard time at this point. She may not be physically ill, but will certainly be struggling to cope with whatever life throws at her. The fullness of the curve of her life line will tell you how well she is able to cope, for a wide and generous curve shows greater resilience in the face of life's obstacles than a moderately curved or straight line.

The color of the line

Look at the color of the life line. Ideally the line should be a moderate pink, as this shows a good level of strength and health. A very pale line indicates a lack of physical stamina. It does not suggest that the person will always be ill, merely that she has limited reserves of energy that are quickly depleted and must be replaced. She needs frequent periods of recuperation. However, a pale line that is also very feathery and weak throughout its length does indicate someone who is often ill. Having read this, you might imagine that a scarlet life line indicates someone who is in the best of health, but in fact it suggests health problems, especially if the fingers look very puffy with tightly stretched shiny skin (as opposed to fingers that are merely well covered with flesh). However, you must resist the urge to make medical diagnoses.

Rising lines

Do any lines rise from the life line and move toward one of the mounts? If so, they show that the person has made a huge effort to express the positive characteristics of that mount. Using the timing techniques will tell you when these efforts took place.

A line rising to the mount of Jupiter shows a powerful urge to improve her circumstances in life. A line rising to the mount of Saturn shows an increased sense of responsibility at that point, perhaps caused by having to cope with a taxing job or having to take care of someone. When a line rises to the mount of Apollo, the person will be successful in an artistic or creative field. A line rising to the

POSSIBLE RISING LINES
a *Rises to the mount of Jupiter*
b *Rises to the mount of Saturn*

mount of Mercury indicates a successful business enterprise, especially if it is involved with communication. However, make sure that you are not confusing a line rising to the mount of Mercury with the Mercury line, which is one of the minor lines explained later in this section (see pages 218–219).

A MISSING LIFE LINE

It is very unusual to find someone whose hand lacks a life line, but it is possible. As you might imagine, this person will not have much physical vitality and stamina, so she will need plenty of rest between periods of exertion. If other indications on the hand suggest it, she will struggle to cope with the day-to-day practicalities of life because she is so dreamy and ungrounded. She is also heavily influenced by other people, so she can be easily manipulated by those who do not have her best interests at heart.

What to look for

- *Where the line starts.*
- *How the line starts.*
- *The curve of the line.*
- *The quality of the line.*
- *The color of the line.*
- *Breaks or marks in the line.*
- *Where the line ends.*
- *How the line ends.*

QUICK REMINDER

Each line symbolizes the quality of energy connected with that line. The clearer and stronger the line, the better the energy of that line flows. A line that is broken, faint or crossed by many small lines is experiencing an interruption to its energy.

THE HEART LINE

STARTS Under the mount of Mercury

ENDS Near the mount of Saturn or mount of Jupiter

INDICATES Emotions, the ability to love and be loved

The heart line always attracts a lot of interest because it describes someone's emotional depth and his ability to love others. It also shows whether he usually has happy emotional experiences or whether his relationships are fraught with problems. The concept of the heart line is easy to grasp, especially if you are new to palmistry, so it is a good line for beginners to study.

THE START OF THE LINE

There is a lot of debate in palmistry circles about where the heart line begins. Some people think it begins on the outer edge of the hand, beneath the mount of Mercury (as described in this book); others believe that it starts on the other side of the hand, usually near the mounts of Jupiter or Saturn. As there are two such distinct schools of thought about this, you might enjoy carrying out your own research to see which theory works best for you.

In this book we are following the notion that the heart line always starts on the outer edge of the palm, which means that its starting position never varies and is not open to interpretation.

POSSIBLE ENDING POINTS

a *Ends on the mount of Saturn*
b *Ends midway between the mounts
   of Saturn and Jupiter*
c *Ends on the mount of Jupiter*
d *Ends on the inner edge of the palm*

*There are no marks or other
interruptions to this heart line,
showing someone who is very
self-sufficient and self-absorbed.*

However, we can learn an enormous amount about the person's emotions during his childhood by studying the quality of the heart line in this part of his hand. The color and strength of the line will also give you valuable information.

Clear and well marked

If the beginning of the heart line is clearly marked, with no stressful lines cutting across it and no other indications of emotional problems, the person had a happy and uncomplicated childhood. Check the beginnings of the other major lines—the life, head and fate lines—to see if they also show this happy start in life. If so, this person certainly had a fortunate childhood and you will want to examine the rest of the heart line to see if this emotionally idyllic state of affairs continues throughout his life. However, do not automatically assume that this happy childhood was the result of family life being almost too perfect for words. It may be because the person learned to shut himself off from the demands and worries of others, so that he was unaffected by anything but his own needs. This could mean he is extremely self-centered, rather than blessed with a happy home life, but you will have to reserve judgment at this stage.

Is the start of the heart line clear on both hands? If so, this person either had an incredibly happy childhood or is completely wrapped up in himself. If the line is only clear on the dominant hand, with stressful lines on the nondominant hand, this shows that he has risen above his early difficulties and may have blocked them out of his conscious mind. If the line is only clear on the nondominant hand, he is idealizing his childhood and imagining that it was much easier than it really was.

Feathered

If the beginning of the heart line is feathered, with lots of small lines running off it, this indicates that the childhood was emotionally difficult. There may have been problems between the person's parents, or the family might have had to cope with traumatic events that threw the whole household into emotional disarray. Do not forget to check the start of the heart line on both hands to see how

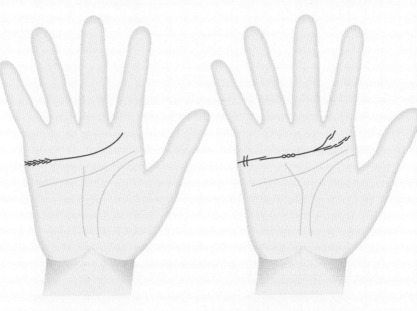

This heart line has a feathered start but it then runs without interruptions.

The energy of this heart line is disrupted throughout its length.

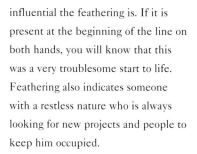

influential the feathering is. If it is present at the beginning of the line on both hands, you will know that this was a very troublesome start to life. Feathering also indicates someone with a restless nature who is always looking for new projects and people to keep him occupied.

Look at the rest of the line to see how long the feathering lasts. You will be coming back to the rest of the line in more detail later, but it is always helpful to gain an overall view of the state of the heart line at an early stage because it is such an important time.

THE END OF THE LINE

Although the heart line has a very definite starting point under the mount of Mercury, it makes up for this by having a variety of end positions. Each such position will tell you a great deal about the person's emotional state, such as whether he is jealous, idealistic, passionate or reserved.

On the side of the palm

When you see a heart line that runs across the entire width of the palm, almost as though it were wrapped around the palm like a piece of string, you know that this person is emotionally greedy. He is someone who wants everything from his partner and is determined to get it. If you are wondering whether to get emotionally involved with someone, you might want to check whether he has this sort of heart line before committing yourself. This type of heart line is very long, which means that he will experience many different emotions throughout his life.

As always when you see anything notable in the hand, you should check whether this very long heart line appears on both hands or just one. When both hands have this marking, the person is in thrall to his powerful emotions. If it is only on his nondominant hand, he has these tendencies, but mostly manages to control them. If a long heart line is present only on the dominant hand, his jealousy cannot help but break through the emotional instincts that are described by his heart line on his nondominant hand.

Under the mount of Jupiter

A heart line ending under the mount of Jupiter belongs to someone who has a tendency to wear rose-colored glasses in his relationships. He will

Here is an example of a very long heart line. It runs right across the palm and ends on the side of the hand.

idealize people, overlooking their negative points until the scales finally fall from his eyes, at which point he will feel bitterly disappointed at discovering that the person in question is human after all. This is always a blow to his pride as well as his heart. Nevertheless, this person has great emotional depth because of the length of his heart line. He is loyal, faithful and his love for partners, friends and family will endure for years—sometimes long after the relationship has ended.

Between the mounts of Jupiter and Saturn

When the heart line ends here, the person in question has the emotional qualities of both of these mounts— that is, he has the emotional depth and loyalty of the mount of Jupiter, but is able to combine these characteristics with the passion and sensuality of the mount of Saturn. He also has the practicality and common sense of Saturn, so is less likely to have his heart broken by putting his loved ones on pedestals.

On the mount of Saturn

The mount of Saturn always shows that things are being taken seriously, so when the heart line ends here, it indicates that the person places a lot of importance on his love life and does his best to ensure that it is a success. He is passionate and highly sexed, and at times his sexual needs will overcome the more rational parts of his personality. This is considered to be a short heart line, which means that he has not experienced as many different emotions as someone with a very long heart line. It may also mean that he always responds in the same way to a certain situation, rather than learning from a difficult experience and responding differently in future to avoid repeating his mistakes.

THE CURVE OF THE LINE

Is the heart line relatively straight, gently curved or very curved? The shape the line makes as it sweeps across the palm tells you how sensitive the person is to the needs of other people.

Normal

The normal heart line is gently curved. This shows someone who is able to meet the needs of other people, but who can also meet his own needs when necessary. In other words he is not completely selfless, but his world does not revolve around himself either.

WAYS THE LINE CAN CURVE
a *Almost straight*
b *Normal*
c *Very curved*

Very curved

If the heart line is very curved—almost like a crescent—the person is highly attuned to the needs and

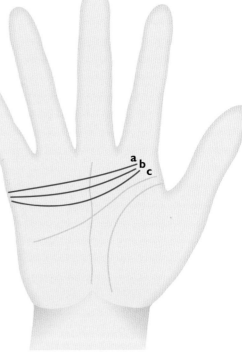

feelings of others. If other factors in his hand emphasize this tendency, he is so sensitive that he is almost like a human barometer, measuring the moods of the people around him.

If such a strongly curved heart line is almost unmarked by small lines (usually the indicator of someone who is self-centered), then the curve of the heart line will help to compensate for the lack of markings.

Almost straight

Sometimes the heart line runs in an almost straight line, with very little curvature at all. A line of this sort belongs to someone who lacks sensitivity about other people's feelings and who has a tendency to suppress his own strong emotions. He may be like an emotional volcano inside, but hates to show it. He is the classic "strong and silent" type. Look to see if the heart line is straight on both hands. If it is, the person has a no-nonsense attitude to love, especially if the line is also short. It is as though he has a limited repertoire of emotions and is unable to experience some feelings at all.

THE POSITION OF THE HEART LINE

Your next step is to examine the position of the heart line on the palm. Look to see if it lies very near the base of the fingers, midway between the fingers and the head line, or much closer to the head line than the fingers.

Normal

The normal position of the heart line is midway between the base of the fingers and the head line. This shows someone who has an average experience of love: not the stuff of fairy tales or particularly exceptional in any way.

This is a very high-set heart line. It sits much closer to the base of the fingers than it does to the head line.

High-set

If the heart line is much closer to the base of the fingers than the head line, it is considered high-set, indicating someone who finds it easy to get along well with others, thanks to his affectionate and open personality. He is also very idealistic about relationships, tending to put partners on pedestals.

This is a very low-set heart line. It drops so far down into the palm that it touches the head line.

Low-set

A low-set heart line is nearest to the head line, and shows someone who tends to bottle up his feelings. He is thoughtful and considerate toward loved ones, but it takes an almost superhuman effort for him to be as demonstrative with them as they would like. Nevertheless, he is often very passionate sexually.

THE REST OF THE LINE

When you start to examine someone's heart line, the first question he will probably ask you is: "Am I lucky in love?" We have already discussed a number of ways to check this, but you also need to look at what happens to the line as it runs along the hand. Are there many breaks or interruptions to it, indicating interruptions to the emotions, or is it smooth along its entire length?

Interruptions to the line

Most of us have a few marks on our heart lines, such as short lines that cross the line at right angles and show interruptions and disturbances to relationships. A severe rift in a relationship, such as a traumatic break-up or parting from a loved one, is indicated by a break in the heart line. Such breaks are discussed later in this section (see pages 240–245), helping you to interpret them in more detail.

Small lines

If there are lots of small lines running off the heart line at an angle, the person is very affectionate and has a knack of making strong emotional contact with others. Tradition says that these relationships are happy if the lines rise upward, and unhappy if they point downward. However, this seems rather a simplistic judgment and you may decide it is more accurate to say that small lines pointing downward to the head line indicate that the person is primarily looking for an intellectual connection with others (especially if the small lines actually meet the head line), and small lines pointing upward show the desire for emotional connections.

Joined lines

Does the heart line touch either the head or life lines at any point? If the heart line dips down so far in the middle of the hand that it touches the

Here, the end of the heart line meets the start of the life and head lines. It is the sign of someone who is controlled by their powerful emotional needs.

life line, it shows someone who has such a powerful need for physical and emotional contact that he will do almost anything to get it. You might want to think twice before getting deeply involved with this person, because you will not know what you are letting yourself in for.

If the end of the heart line joins the start of the head and life lines near the thumb, you may want to give this person a wide berth too. He finds it very difficult to separate his emotions from his thoughts and actions, so there is very little to stop him doing exactly what he wants, especially if he has a weak thumb.

The color of the line

Always check the color of the heart line—it should be a good color that complements the rest of the hand. A pale heart line on a well-colored palm shows someone whose emotions do not flow well or are repressed. A very red heart line on a pale palm indicates someone who experiences powerful emotions that can get out of control at times.

A MISSING HEART LINE

People are able to survive perfectly well if their heart line is missing, although they may not experience very deep emotions. Sometimes, however, the heart line is not really missing, but has fused along its entire

---

What to look for

- *How the line starts.*
- *The curve of the line.*
- *The quality of the line.*
- *The color of the line.*
- *Breaks or marks in the line.*
- *Where the line ends.*
- *How the line ends.*

length with the head line. This is
called a simian line and is discussed
in detail later on (see pages 214–215).

When is a fork not a fork?

*There are times when it is difficult to
see whether the heart line has ended
in a fork or whether it has been
crossed by a subsidiary line.
Sometimes you can trace the
so-called fork down the hand and
discover that it is connected to a
small line; this means it is not a
fork, but a line. Alternatively, closer
inspection (perhaps with a
magnifying glass) may reveal that
the two lines are not joined, in which
case you are looking at a fork after
all. When the heart line ends in a
fork, you can analyze it by looking at
where each prong of the fork leads.
So if one prong ends on the mount of
Jupiter and the other on the mount
of Saturn, the person's emotional
make-up is a mixture of the
optimism and idealism of the mount
of Jupiter and the seriousness of the
mount of Saturn.*

THE HEAD LINE

STARTS Near the thumb, between the heart and life lines

ENDS Below the heart line under the mount of Mercury

INDICATES Intellect and the ability to think clearly

For many palmists, the head line is the most important line on the palm because it describes someone's level of intelligence, the way she thinks and her ability to convey her thoughts to other people. After all, successful communication is an essential part of life, and it is difficult to make your way in the world if you cannot connect with other people.

THE START OF THE LINE

The head line always begins on the side of the palm near the thumb, although it will start in one of three different positions. The starting point

will tell you a great deal about the person's thought processes and the usual path that her thoughts take, so it pays to study it carefully. As with all the other lines on the hand, you need to compare the start of the head lines on the right and left hands. Do they differ in some way? Is one much stronger than the other? Do they begin in different places, or are there other notable differences in the way they begin? For instance, the head line on the nondominant palm may begin closer to the heart line than it does on the dominant palm, in which case the person has learned to put a

POSSIBLE STARTING POINTS
a *Starts on the mount of Jupiter*
b *Joined to the life line*
c *Starts beneath the life line*

brave face on her emotional disappointments.

There is no "normal" position for the start of the head line. It starts in one of three positions: on the mount of Jupiter; joined to the life line; or beneath the life line, although you will find variations within these.

On the mount of Jupiter

When the head line begins here, it shows someone who is confident and ambitious. She is well aware of her abilities and takes pride in a good job well done. If the line starts very high on the mount of Jupiter (perhaps almost touching the finger of Jupiter), the person is trustworthy to a fault.

Look to see how big the gap is between the start of the head and life lines. The bigger the space between them, the more impatient and impulsive the person is—she has always liked to think for herself, even from an early age.

Joined to the life line

When the head and life lines begin together, the person lacks confidence in her ability to make important decisions and always likes to get a second opinion before committing herself. It is therefore hardly a surprise that she is cautious, not very independent and strongly influenced by her family. Look to see whether the two lines are joined for only a short distance or much farther, because the length of fusion of the two lines will show you how long the influence will last. How soon will this person be able to cut the apron strings, or will she remain tied to her family for most of her life?

Beneath the life line

When the head line starts below the life line, on the mount of Venus itself, it shows someone who is very unsure of her place in the world. She needs continual reassurance that she is on the right track, and is wary of sticking her neck out in any way. She is shy and timid, and likes to keep a low profile.

THE END OF THE LINE

The end of the line is just as informative as its beginning. The

This head line curves right down to end on the mount of the Moon. It is a sign of strong imagination but also possible depressive tendencies.

head line can end at any point from the outer edge of the palm down to the mount of the Moon. Examine the end of the line carefully to see what it looks like. Does it end in a fork or tassel? Does it curve upward or downward, or does it do something else? You may need to use your

A writer's fork, which is the term given to the forked end of a head line, denotes the ability to think objectively.

magnifying glass to see exactly what is happening if the person's hand is covered with small lines.

Writer's fork

If the head line ends in a simple fork, this is known as a "writer's fork." It shows that the person has the ability to see more than one point of view, which can be very useful for a writer. However, it is not just writers who have such forks on their hands, and being able to appreciate both sides of a question can be a useful talent in many walks of life.

Large fork

Sometimes the head line ends in a pronounced fork, with one end of the line stretching out toward the percussion and the other dipping down toward the mount of the Moon. This shows that the person is able to combine practicality (shown by the line moving toward the percussion) with imagination (shown by the line stretching toward the mount of the Moon). Look to see if both ends of the fork are equally strong or whether one is more pronounced than the other. For instance, if the part of the fork heading toward the mount of the Moon is strongest, that person's imagination exerts more control over her than her practical streak.

Tassel

A line that ends in a tassel shows someone who will have several interests at the end of her life. Look to see if any line of the tassel is stronger than the others; if so, notice which direction it points in, because this will tell you which interest will be most important to her.

Upward curve

Does the line end in an upward curve, almost like a little hook, that points toward one of the fingers? If so, the person's mind is influenced by the area of life ruled by that finger. For instance, if the curve points toward the Mercury finger, she is influenced by her connections with other people, so other people's words and ideas may carry a lot of weight for her. If the curve points toward the Apollo finger, it is her own creative abilities that influence her thoughts. Check to see if this curve is present on both palms and, if so, whether it ends under the same fingers.

THE QUALITY OF THE LINE

Does the head line look strong or weak? Is it deeply etched, well drawn or very fine? There is a simple rule to remember when examining the head line: the clearer the line, the clearer the person's thoughts. So a very clear line shows someone who thinks in a straightforward and logical way. She is a good speaker who finds it easy to express herself, and may also have the ability to hit the nail on the head when talking.

Any breaks, chains or islands that appear on the line act as interruptions to the person's thought processes. If someone's head line is full of chains, her thoughts tend to go round in circles and it is difficult for her to think clearly. When you talk to her, her conversation rambles all over the place and at times you may even wonder if she will ever reach the point of her story. If the chains only appear on a small stretch of the line, she will experience a period of confusion and muddled thinking during the time scale indicated by the position of the chains on the line. You will learn how to time events shown in the lines later in this section (see pages 246–249).

THE DISTANCE BETWEEN THE HEAD AND HEART LINES

Something else to look for is the space separating the head and heart

There is a large gap in this palm between the middle of the heart and head lines. It shows a great tolerance for other people's foibles.

POSSIBLE ENDING POINTS

a *Ends on the plain of Mars
beneath the Mercury finger*

b *Ends near the percussion*

c *Ends beneath the Apollo finger*

d *Ends beneath the Saturn finger*

lines along their length. Even if the lines are close together at first, they will move apart at some point (unless they have formed a simian line; see pages 214–215) and you need to establish how much distance there is between them.

If only a short distance separates the head and heart lines, the person is cautious, reserved and withdrawn. She is very private and it will take a lot for her to confide in others, because she likes to keep herself to herself. This is especially true if the head and life lines are joined at the start.

A large gap between the head and heart lines denotes someone who is broad-minded and unconventional. It takes a lot to shock her, because she has such a tolerant attitude to life.

THE LENGTH OF THE LINE

How long is the head line on each palm? Is one shorter than the other? The length of the line will give you more information about what the person thinks about and how she expresses herself. Nevertheless, a short head line does not mean poor brain power or below-average intelligence, and when you find a long head line it does not mean that you are holding the hand of a genius.

Normal

The head line usually ends at some point on the plain of Mars beneath the Mercury or little finger, indicating someone whose thinking processes take an average length of time: She does not leap to instant conclusions, but does not mull things over for hours, either. She has a normal amount of imagination, without going to extremes in either direction.

Long

When the head line ends near the percussion, the person thinks things through in great detail. She likes to mull problems over in her own time, sifting through her options and not reaching a conclusion until she is satisfied that she has considered every angle. She also has a strong imagination, which of course may interfere with her thought processes by introducing lots of other possibilities that she will then want to consider in her own time.

Short

A head line that ends under the finger of Apollo shows someone who makes up her mind in an instant. She reacts quickly and always approaches situations from a practical viewpoint. In fact, she can become irritable with people whose brains do not operate as quickly as hers, or who take time to reach decisions.

Sometimes you will see a very short head line that ends under the finger of Saturn. Remember, this does not indicate a lack of intelligence.

The person does, however, lack imagination and will fail to see why everyone else cannot think in the same way she does. She does not have much patience either, and may lack common sense.

THE SHAPE OF THE LINE

One of the most telling features of the head line is its shape as it runs across the palm. Is it so straight that it looks as though it has been drawn with a ruler? Is it wavy, with lots of ups and downs? Or is it curved? Each of these shapes tells you about the way that person's mind works.

Straight

When the head line is very straight and runs right across the palm, the person's thoughts run in an equally straight and direct line. She has plenty of common sense and practicality, and takes an objective view of life.

*This is an example of a
very straight head line. It
indicates an ability to think
straight and not be swayed
by subjective considerations.*

The more pronounced the curve of the head line, the more active the person's imagination.

Wavy

If the head line wobbles about, almost as if it does not know which direction it is going in, the person has a very inventive and unusual mind. She is unconventional and original, but can have problems in reaching decisions because so many different options are open to her.

Curved

When the head line is curved, she is highly imaginative. Look to see whether the line is curved on both hands. If it is curved on the nondominant hand and straight on the dominant one, it denotes someone who tries to curb her imagination, perhaps because her job requires her to be highly practical or because she has been brought up to smother inventive thinking. When you find the reverse, with the curved line on the dominant hand, she has actively developed her imagination.

Sloping

Look to see if the head line slopes downward, because this is another indication of imagination. When the downward slope is very obvious, the person has a powerful imagination. If the head line runs down into the mount of the Moon, she has a tendency to let her imagination run away with her, conjuring up pessimistic thoughts and fears about the worst possible things that can happen to her. This is especially likely if it is confirmed by other features on her hands.

THE REST OF THE LINE

Now it is time to examine the entire head line. Look along its length to see whether it changes color or strength at any point, as these changes in its condition will show times of mental stress and pressure.

Lines of interference

Are there any lines crossing the head line? Such lines are called "lines of interference" because they block the energy represented by the line. So lines that run across the head line will show times when the person's ideas are influenced by outside people or situations.

Fuzziness

Is the line clear, or is it blurred and fuzzy? If it is blurred, almost as though it has been smudged, it shows that the person is easily distracted and finds it difficult to concentrate on anything for long. If the line is only fuzzy for a short while, she will go through a phase when she lacks concentration; if it is fuzzy along its entire length, she will always struggle to control her mind and stop it wandering off whenever she gets bored.

Branches

Does the head line branch out at any point? We have already talked about forks at the end of the line, but are there any forks or branches before the end of the line? If so, where do they lead and how strong are they? Any branches that lead off the line indicate new areas of interest that the person has explored, and you will be able to

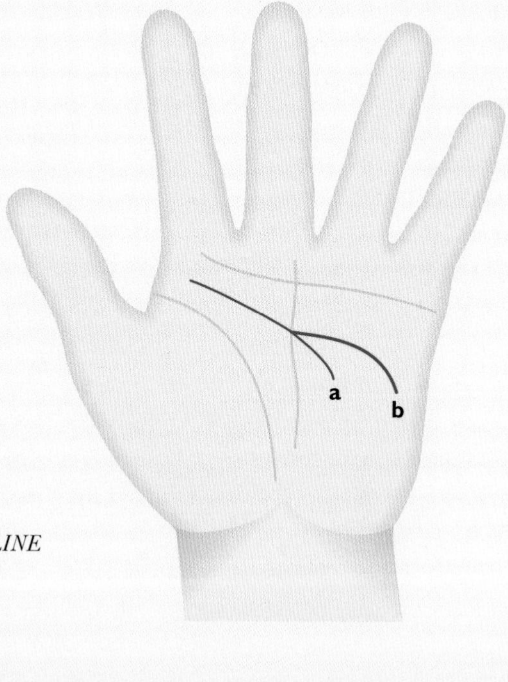

BRANCHING HEAD LINE
a *Original line*
b *Stronger branch*

tell by their condition whether these interests continued or were abandoned. For instance, branches that lead from the head line to the heart line show interests that have completely captivated her imagination and her heart. If the branch becomes stronger than the head line itself, her original ideas and convictions will be superseded by new ways of thinking at the point in her life indicated by the beginning of the branch.

A MISSING HEAD LINE

Every now and then you will come across a hand where there is only one line running across the palm and you are unsure whether it is the head or heart line. When this happens, the lines have joined together to form a simian line. The meaning of this line is explained in detail later in this section (see pages 214–215).

HEAD LINE VERSUS LIFE LINE

Compare the condition of the head line with that of the life line. Is one stronger or more defined than the other? If the head line is the stronger line, that person's inner life and her thoughts and ideas will always have more importance for her than her outer circumstances.

What to look for

- *Where the line starts.*
- *The quality of the line.*
- *The distance between the head and heart lines.*
- *The length of the line.*
- *The shape of the line.*
- *Where the line ends.*
- *How the line ends.*

THE FATE LINE

STARTS At the base of the palm

ENDS Near the finger of Saturn

INDICATES Worldly affairs, career, the direction of life

The fate line is one of the most fascinating lines on the palm because it shows the path our lives take, with the major ups and downs that may occur and the influence that other people have on us. It also says a great deal about the direction our lives will take, and whether we will always pursue the same interests and jobs or whether these will change at some point.

THE START OF THE LINE

There is no "normal" start to the fate line, but it always begins in one of three places: on the mount of Venus, between the mount of Venus and the mount of the Moon, and on the mount of the Moon. You will also see variations in the position at which the fate line starts on the palm, with some lines beginning at the very base of the wrist and others starting much farther up. All these positions mean something, as you will soon discover.

On the mount of Venus

If the fate line begins on the mount of Venus, either beside or tucked behind the life line, it shows that the person has been strongly influenced by his early upbringing and family background. It is highly likely that he

POSSIBLE STARTING POSITIONS

a *Starts inside the life line*
b *Starts next to the life line*
c *Starts between the life line and the mount of the Moon*
d *Starts on the mount of the Moon*
e *Starts high up the palm*

has fulfilled his family's expectations, perhaps because he was told to follow in the footsteps of one of his parents. For instance, you would expect to see this fate line on someone who has joined the family firm or become a doctor, because that was the dearest wish of his parents. He is conventional and cautious, especially if the fate line starts behind the life line. This person will only manage to extract himself from his family's powerful influence when the fate line moves away from the life line.

Between the mounts of Venus and the Moon

When the fate line starts in the middle of the palm, between the mounts of Venus and the Moon, the person has found a good balance between being strongly influenced by his family and being determined to do his own thing. If he is doing a job that runs in the family, he will have chosen it because he loves it, rather than because it was expected of him. He also treads a middle ground between being highly conventional and highly unconventional.

On the mount of the Moon

When the fate line begins here, the person has always made his own decisions about what he wants to do with his life, rather than being influenced by other people. His choice of career, or the path he takes through life, is individual and imaginative, and often it has a creative slant that may take many forms. He also needs to work with other people, rather than completely on his own, and is therefore much happier as part of a team because he needs the stimulus of bouncing his ideas off other people. If his job is boring, it is essential for this person to have a rewarding hobby that gives him the creative and emotional satisfaction he does not get from his working life, otherwise he will feel that something is seriously missing from his life.

The starting position

Does the fate line start at the very base of the palm or farther up? The nearer the beginning of the line to the wrist, the earlier this person's ambitions were kindled. If his fate line starts at the very base of the mount of the Moon, he will have followed his creative ambitions from an early age. If a painter has this marking, for instance, he would have started painting almost as soon as he could hold a brush and would always have wanted to be a painter. His direction in life is like a vocation, even if he has to earn his daily bread doing something else.

If there is quite a distance between the base of the wrist and the start of the fate line, the person is a late-starter who takes a while to discover his purpose in life. There may be many reasons for this, from confusion to family restrictions. The quality and direction of his fate line will tell you whether he finds the right niche for himself.

THE END OF THE LINE

Look to see where the fate line ends. It can end in one of several places, all of which will tell you how the person's career or vocation will end. Will his job last to the end of his life? Will it stop when he retires, or will something else happen? The end of the fate line will give you plenty of information about this.

On the heart line

The heart line is the classic stopping place for someone whose job ends when he retires and who does not take up any further interests after this point. Maybe his idea of bliss is to potter about in the garden, avoiding any activities that will be a drain on his time. Check carefully to see that the

POSSIBLE ENDING POINTS
a *Ends at the head line*
b *Ends at the heart line*
c *Ends on the mount of Jupiter*
d *Ends on the mount of Saturn*

*In this palm the start
of the fate line is tucked
inside the life line. It
ends when it meets the
head line and is therefore
quite short.*

fate line does not form a small branch when it appears to end at the heart line, as this will indicate that the person develops another active interest after retirement. If a new line seems to grow after the original one stopped at the heart line, he will develop a new interest that he really loves and in which he will become deeply

involved. If this new line ends on the mount of Jupiter, he will become so engrossed that he seems to eat, sleep and drink this interest.

On the head line

The fate line is considered to be short if it ends here. It shows someone who loses direction and purpose in life after reaching the age at which the fate line ends: usually his late thirties or early forties. He may drift through life after this, or take a series of jobs that are more about paying the bills than giving him any sort of satisfaction. Once again, you should avoid viewing his situation subjectively, especially if you are strongly focused on your own career or your life's purpose. Perhaps this person had a highly demanding job until his early forties, working on the stock exchange, in a hospital or somewhere equally stressful, and now wants to avoid all job responsibility because he feels he deserves a rest. Alternatively, he will try and fail to find a sense of satisfaction in what he does after his forties. This, of course, is a rather gloomy prognostication, so be careful how you phrase it. You should also remember that lines can change, and so the person may work hard at developing other interests, which will then be shown in the lines in his hands.

On the mount of Saturn

When the fate line ends here, the person will remain heavily involved in his job, or other interests, until his death. If the fate line starts low on the mount of the Moon, you can safely assume that this person has a strong creative streak, which he will want to express during the whole of his life. There is no such thing as complete retirement for him, because he will always be actively involved in something that captures his interest and imagination.

On the mount of Jupiter

This is someone with very strong ambitions, who will do his utmost to realize them. He will achieve his goals somehow, no matter how long it takes. A marking of this kind indicates such powerful drive and

This fate line starts on the mount of the Moon and ends on the mount of Saturn, showing a lifelong sense of purpose.

motivation that he will almost inevitably make a name for himself in his chosen field. However, his occupation will be an all-consuming interest rather than a nine-to-five job, so he may neglect other areas of his life through lack of time.

THE QUALITY OF THE LINE

What does the fate line look like? Remember that it describes someone's purpose and direction in life, not only in his career, but in every other sphere of his life as well. This is highly subjective, of course,

This is a weak, meandering fate line, showing someone who finds it hard to stick with anything for long.

because what suits one person may not suit another. You must realize that we all have different ideas of what success means: for one person, it may mean enjoying a happy family life, while another person may only consider himself a success when he has earned his first million.

The simple rule to bear in mind is that a clear line indicates a settled direction in life. So the more strongly marked the fate line is, the stronger that person's sense of purpose and direction. If he is lucky, he will be happy about this. But what does it mean if his fate line began tucked behind his life line and continues in a straight line up his hand? Does it mean he will spend his life feeling that he has no choice but to follow in the family footsteps? Ask him, and listen carefully to the answer, because it will increase your knowledge of palmistry.

When you find a weak, faint or wavering fate line, the person is unsure of his direction in life. He will struggle to express what he feels is his life's purpose, or may never get a sense of what this actually is. Examine the rest of his hand to see if you can discover why this should be.

THE RIGHT AND LEFT PALMS

As with every other line on the hand, it is important to examine both palms to see how the lines differ. Often you will find that the fate line on the nondominant hand is much weaker than that on the dominant hand. This shows the person makes a great effort to realize his vague dreams and aspirations. If the fate line is stronger on the nondominant hand, he has all sorts of wonderful ideas that never see the light of day.

You will probably find many other differences between the fate lines on the right and left palms. For instance, they may start or end in different places, or one line may have more forks and branches than the other. Examine all these differences carefully, as they have a story to tell you.

FORKS AND BRANCHES

Does the fate line fork anywhere? Look carefully, especially if the person has a water hand covered with lots of small subsidiary lines which can be confusing. Make sure you look at the whole of the fate line, rather than just the start and end, otherwise you might miss something. You must also pay particular attention to lines that branch out where the fate line meets the head or heart lines, because these can look like separate lines until you study them carefully and realize that they are joined to the fate line.

When you do find a fork, it shows the point at which the person takes up more than one interest or career. If the fate line ends in a small fork, the number of prongs of the fork indicates the number of different interests that he will have at the end of his life. So four prongs will show four interests.

If the fork is long enough to form a branch, with lines leading to different mounts, the person's life will involve experiences that are influenced by the mounts in question. For instance, a branching fate line that reaches to the

Be tactful

Always choose your words carefully and with tact when you are delivering what might be construed as bad news. If someone's fate line is littered with lines of interference, symbolizing many blockages to his path through life, be careful how you phrase this. You must not scare him or project your own fears on to his situation—you might be frightened by the sort of challenges that he will relish.

BRANCHING FATE LINE

a *Branch leading to the mount of Jupiter*

b *Branch leading to the mount of Saturn*

*This fate line ends in a
three-pronged fork, with the
left-hand branch much
stronger than the other two.*

Jupiter and Saturn mounts shows someone who will work to the end of his life (shown by the branch leading to the Saturn mount) in a career or interest that puts him in the public eye or gives him a lot of power (shown by the Jupiter mount). You will be able to interpret any branches if you consider the basic meanings of the mounts and adapt them to the life of the person in question.

THE REST OF THE LINE

Take a look at the fate line as a whole. Is it easy to see, or do you have to peer into the palm to spot it? Remember, the more definite the fate line is, the stronger that person's drive.

Lines of interference

Look to see if there are any lines of interference running horizontally across the fate line on either hand. These lines indicate times of stress and difficulty, when the person meets

---

Palmistry case study

The fate line on Sarah's dominant palm is in three separate sections, with the end of each section overlapping the start of the next one. This shows that her working life has been split into three distinct chapters, with each new chapter beginning before the old one has come to an end. Sure enough, she has eased herself gradually into each new chapter, often without realizing what was happening to her.

---

an obstacle that seems to block his progress. You can use the method of timing events on the lines, described later in this section (see pages 246–249), to establish when these obstacles will occur in that person's life. Check whether the lines occur at

*Many lines of interference
block the energy of this fate
line. However, the line is
clearer after it has passed
the head line.*

the same point on both palms, because if they do, these indicate serious obstacles that he has to grapple with. Does a line run off the obstacle line, thereby forming a small branch? If so, look to see where it leads, because this will give you clues about how he can navigate his way round the obstacle.

A MISSING FATE LINE

If the fate line is missing on one or both palms, it does not mean that the person has no fate. Instead, it shows that he prefers to take life as it comes rather than plan it in advance. Check carefully to make sure there really is no fate line, because sometimes it is so faint that it is difficult to see at first, or it may look as though it is masquerading as a completely different line.

Sometimes it is hard to see the fate line because it is broken and the pieces do not appear to relate to each other.

What to look for
- *Where the line starts.*
- *The quality of the line.*
- *The right and left palms.*
- *Forks and branches.*
- *Where the line ends.*
- *How the line ends.*

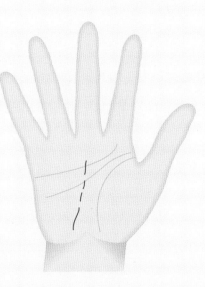

THE SIMIAN LINE

STARTS   Between the thumb and Jupiter finger

ENDS   On or near the outer palm

INDICATES   A merging of intellectual and emotional
energy, so there is no division between thoughts and feelings

The simian line is considered to be a major line, although most hands do not have one. When it does appear, it replaces the head and heart lines. A simian line is striking because it cuts straight across the palm and usually appears midway between the position that the head and heart lines would have occupied, if they were present on the hand. It is a fusion of the head and heart lines, which means that the person's emotional and mental energies work together, and she throws herself wholeheartedly into life. She cannot tell the difference between her thoughts and her emotions.

SETTING

If the simian line is set low on the hand, that person experiences strong emotional compulsions that override her common sense; if it is set higher on the hand, nearer the Jupiter finger than the thumb, she is more able to reason with herself and can therefore behave with greater objectivity.

ONE OR BOTH HANDS?

Look to see whether the simian line appears on both hands or only one. It is very rare to find it on both hands, when it indicates someone who is completely unable to separate her

This is a classic example of a simian line, where the heart and head lines have merged into a single line.

emotions and ideas. This person is driven by instinct and belief, and may be capable of extreme reactions. She is often immensely creative.

When the simian line appears only on the nondominant hand, she has an erratic attitude to life. Sometimes she channels all her energy into it, and at other times she is content to coast along. When the simian line appears only on the dominant hand, she is well aware of the dynamic (and sometimes provocative or disturbing) effect that she has on others.

THE MINOR LINES OF THE HAND

Although you may already have been familiar with the major lines of the palm before you started to read this book, you may not know the minor lines. These lines are not present on every hand, but when they do appear they give us interesting information. Although they are called "minor," they are important because they help to describe someone's personality.

Study your own hands for these minor lines so that you can become accustomed to their shape and position. Do not forget to look at both your right and left palms. It is not always easy to spot some of these lines because, especially on a water hand that is covered with fine lines, at first sight they may masquerade as something else. For instance, a Mercury or Apollo line may look more like a branch from the line of fate, until you study the hand more closely. Always work in a good light, otherwise you may miss some important lines or misread them.

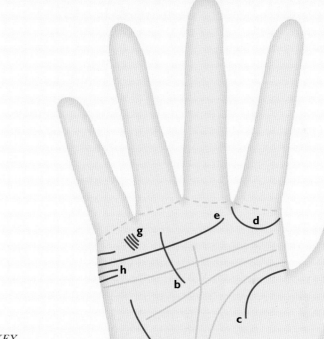

KEY

a *The line of Mercury*
b *The line of Apollo*
c *The line of Mars*
d *The ring of Solomon*
e *The girdle of Venus*
f *The bracelets of Neptune*
g *The medical stigmata*
h *The lines of marriage*

THE LINE OF MERCURY

STARTS At the base of the palm

ENDS Somewhere below the mount of Mercury

INDICATES Health and general constitution

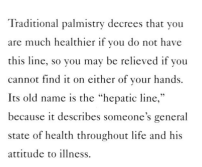

Traditional palmistry decrees that you are much healthier if you do not have this line, so you may be relieved if you cannot find it on either of your hands. Its old name is the "hepatic line," because it describes someone's general state of health throughout life and his attitude to illness.

STRONG LINE

As with most of the other lines on the hand, it is preferable to have a strong Mercury line rather than a weak one, because it indicates that the person in question has a good constitution. He is able to cope with pressure without becoming ill or exhausted.

WEAK LINE

A weak, fragmented, thin or wavering line indicates someone whose health is not as robust as it could be, and who may even have phases of being a complete hypochondriac. He should take extra care of himself whenever he is under pressure, because his body will soon start to show the strain. Ask him if he has a particular weak spot in his body, such as his throat or stomach, which acts as an early-warning alarm when he has pushed himself too far. He should pay attention to this part of the body and do his best to relax whenever it threatens to act up. He should also realize that he does not have as much stamina as he thinks and therefore needs plenty of rest and good food.

STRESS INDICATOR

Some people talk about being stressed all the time, but do they really mean it? You can tell by studying the palm and looking for the line of Mercury, because its presence shows someone who does not handle stress very well.

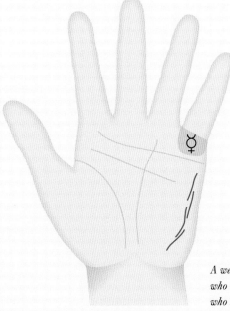

> ### Expert tip
> *Never scare someone by making dire prognostications about his health—or lack of it. You must also avoid diagnosing health problems or telling someone which medicines to take or stop taking.*

A weak line of Mercury indicates someone who needs to take care of their health and who struggles to cope in a crisis.

THE LINE OF APOLLO

STARTS Near the base of the wrist or anywhere on the plain of Mars

ENDS On the mount of Apollo

INDICATES Creative gifts, success, strong motivation

Also known as the line of the Sun, the Apollo line is traditionally believed to confer great things, such as success and public acclaim, when it appears on a hand. However, in practice it denotes creativity, plus the capacity to be happy and to put plenty of energy into life. This is definitely one form of success, although many people with

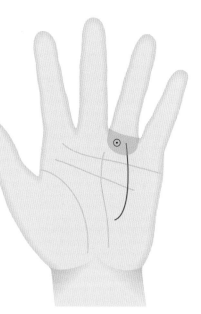

A strong line of Apollo, showing success, is always a welcome sign on a palm.

Apollo lines will never be famous. Instead, they are happy with what they achieve.

FINDING THE LINE

Just as it can be difficult to find buried treasure, so it can be hard to locate the line of Apollo on a hand, because it is so easily mistaken for other lines. Life is made easier if both the lines of Apollo and Mercury are present on the hand, because then there is no danger of you mistaking one for the other. However, if only one of these lines is present, you will have to decide which one it is.

STARTING POINT

Sometimes the line of Apollo begins near or on the base of the wrist and moves straight up the palm toward the mount of Apollo, indicating someone who will enjoy plenty of success during her life, but will have to work for it. If the Apollo line

Expert tip
If you cannot find the line of Apollo, it helps to look first at the mount of Apollo, where the line always ends, and then trace any lines downward through the palm.

begins on or near the life line, it shows that she will enjoy the support of influential people throughout her life. When it begins on or near the head line, she has strong motivation to succeed in life; when it begins on or near the heart line, she will channel great emotional energy into achieving her goals.

THE LINE OF MARS

STARTS Between the life line and the thumb

ENDS On the mount of Venus

INDICATES Good health, energy and talent

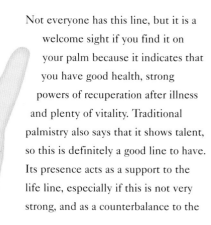

Not everyone has this line, but it is a welcome sight if you find it on your palm because it indicates that you have good health, strong powers of recuperation after illness and plenty of vitality. Traditional palmistry also says that it shows talent, so this is definitely a good line to have. Its presence acts as a support to the life line, especially if this is not very strong, and as a counterbalance to the

Here is a good example of a line of Mars, starting beneath the life line and running halfway down the mount of Venus.

low vitality indicated by a weak Mercury line. If the life line is well-developed and strong, a Mars line will be an added bonus, denoting great vitality. However, if you do not have a line of Mars on either hand, this does not necessarily mean that you lack health and talent.

FINDING THE LINE

As with many of the minor lines, it can be difficult to locate the Mars line on a palm until you are fairly practiced in the art of palmistry. Make sure you do not confuse it with a double life line, which runs much closer to the life line than the Mars line. Study the palm in a good light and look for a short line that begins roughly midway between the life line and the start of the thumb. It will normally curve down the mount of Venus for a short distance, although occasionally you will see a Mars line that extends much farther than this, down to the base of the mount of Venus. Look to see if the line is stronger on one hand than on the other.

ONE OR BOTH HANDS?

As always, look at each hand to see if the line of Mars is present on both of them. Since this line strengthens the life line, it is a particularly favorable sign if it appears on both the right and left hands.

> ### Expert tip
> *If you are struggling to locate the line of Mars in someone's palm, ask him to cup his hand gently, which will emphasize the lines on his palm. If the line of Mars is present, it will show up as a definite crease.*

THE RING OF SOLOMON

WHERE Around the mount of Jupiter

INDICATES An ability to tune in to other people, an instinctive understanding of them, counseling skills

In traditional palmistry, the ring of Solomon is said to denote psychic gifts and the ability to know what other people are thinking. It is therefore an ideal mark for someone who wants to work psychically, perhaps as a clairvoyant. However, the ring of Solomon is also excellent for someone whose job involves working closely with other people, such as a

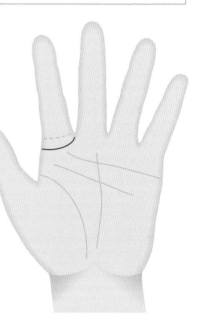

A ring of Solomon encircles the mount of Jupiter and shows empathy for others.

psychotherapist or counselor, because it shows that she has a natural ability to tune in to other people and empathize with them.

FINDING THE LINE

As with every other line on the hand, it is important to know what you are looking for. The ring of Solomon curves around the base of the Jupiter finger or around the mount of Jupiter. It may form a solid semicircle, or only part of it may be present. Make sure you do not confuse it with the line that marks the point where the Jupiter finger joins the palm: you will find the ring of Solomon farther down the mount of Jupiter than this.

ONE OR BOTH HANDS?

Check to see if the ring of Solomon is present on both hands. If it is, the person has a natural warmth and compassion, and is probably the recipient of many people's confidences and secrets. If the ring is present only on the nondominant hand, her instinctive empathy and sensitivity toward others have been curbed, perhaps through unfortunate experiences in which she felt someone was taking advantage of her. If the ring is present only on the dominant hand, it shows someone who has made a great effort to become more understanding of others.

Expert tip

The ring of Solomon can be an indication of teaching ability, because it shows that the person can establish strong connections with other people.

THE GIRDLE OF VENUS

STARTS On the mount of Jupiter or Saturn

ENDS On the mount of Apollo or Mercury

INDICATES Passion, charm, flirtatiousness, moodiness, emotional sensitivity

This is a minor line that shows passion in someone. It may not necessarily be sexual passion, although this is a strong possibility, but could be passion for a particular hobby or activity, or for an occupation. In other words, someone with a girdle of Venus will put a lot of emotional energy into whatever interests him. He is also highly strung.

FINDING THE LINE

You will find the line, if it exists on the palm, forming a curve between the base of the fingers and the heart line.

Take care not to confuse it with a double heart line, which has a different meaning. The girdle of Venus may be so strongly marked along its length that it looks like a major line, or it may be so fragmented and broken that it seems to appear and disappear.

STRONG LINE

The rule in palmistry is usually that strong lines are more positive than weak ones. However, with the girdle of Venus it is a different story, because a strong, unbroken line indicates someone who is easily affected emotionally by outer events and may be thrown off course as a result. He is very flirtatious, which can cause problems in his relationships. He may also have exaggerated moods, with extreme highs and lows.

WEAK LINE

When the girdle of Venus is broken or patchy, the person has better control of his emotional reactions. He is still sensitive, but not to the extent of someone with a strong girdle of Venus.

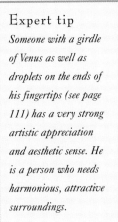

Expert tip

Someone with a girdle of Venus as well as droplets on the ends of his fingertips (see page 111) has a very strong artistic appreciation and aesthetic sense. He is a person who needs harmonious, attractive surroundings.

This girdle of Venus is broken in three places, indicating a healthy amount of emotional energy.

THE BRACELETS OF NEPTUNE

WHERE   At the point where the palm meets the wrist

INDICATE   Good fortune, health

Traditional palmistry teaches that the bracelets of Neptune rule good fortune, so the more bracelets you have, the luckier you are. Contemporary palmistry believes that they show the state of your health. Ideally, you should have two or more bracelets that are strongly marked, and which run straight across the wrist.

FINDING THE LINES

It is easiest to see the bracelets when the wrist is bent inward slightly, so that the lines are emphasized. Now look at the base of the palm, where it joins the wrist. You will see at least one crease, or bracelet of Neptune, that marks this point.

Look for the top bracelet of Neptune nearest the palm. On some hands it can be hard to tell the difference between a broken bracelet and lines that are curving around the base of the mount of Venus, so study this part of the wrist carefully.

THE TOP BRACELET

The top bracelet of Neptune is the most important one, because it tells you about someone's health and stamina. A strong, unbroken and straight bracelet means good health, whereas a chained or broken bracelet indicates a lack of stamina and the need to take care of the health. This is especially true if the bracelet arches up into the base of the wrist, because that suggests problems with the internal organs.

THE OTHER BRACELETS

If the top bracelet is broken or arches upward, it is important to check the state of the other bracelets. If they are straight and unbroken, the health warnings carried in the top bracelet are not as serious as they are if the other bracelets follow the arched or fragmented shape of the top bracelet.

> ### Expert tip
> *Be responsible when assessing someone's health. Do not scare her by uttering dire pronouncements about her state of health, or by making medical diagnoses.*

The top bracelet of Neptune is broken and curved, indicating health problems.

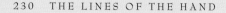
THE MEDICAL STIGMATA

WHERE On the mount of Mercury

INDICATE The ability to help others

When these lines appear on a hand, they signify someone who has an instinctive ability and yearning to help others, especially through one of the healing professions. Although their name may suggest otherwise, the medical stigmata have no connection with that person's own health or medical history.

The medical stigmata consist of a small cluster of short vertical lines on the mount of Mercury.

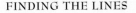

FINDING THE LINES

Examine the hand in a good light, because then you will be certain of seeing the lines if they exist. Do not forget to look at both palms in case the stigmata are present only on the nondominant hand—in which case that person has an urge to help others, but has blocked it for some reason.

The medical stigmata consist of between three and seven short, vertical lines on the mount of Mercury, above the heart line. Check that you are not looking at lines rising from the heart line, or at any other formation of lines, because that will mislead you. Also check the other mounts on the hand in case each one is covered with short vertical lines. If so, it is highly unlikely that those on the mount of Mercury are medical stigmata.

Expert tip

When you find the medical stigmata on someone's hand, you will know that this person has a natural ability and need to help others. He may do this professionally, perhaps through one of the medical professions or as a psychotherapist, or simply by being the sort of person to whom everyone turns in times of trouble. He may work in conventional or complementary medicine, although anyone who has chosen the medical profession purely because of the power and money it can bring them will not have the stigmata on his hands.

THE LINES OF MARRIAGE

WHERE On the side of the hand beneath the finger of Mercury

INDICATE Long-term and important relationships

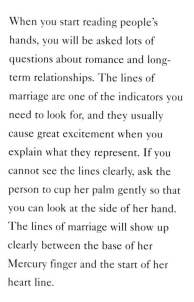

When you start reading people's hands, you will be asked lots of questions about romance and long-term relationships. The lines of marriage are one of the indicators you need to look for, and they usually cause great excitement when you explain what they represent. If you cannot see the lines clearly, ask the person to cup her palm gently so that you can look at the side of her hand. The lines of marriage will show up clearly between the base of her Mercury finger and the start of her heart line.

Although they are called "lines of marriage," they do not relate solely to marriages. Instead, they indicate serious relationships that have had such an impact on the person concerned that they are shown in her hand. This explains why sometimes you will come across someone whose marriages outnumber her marriage lines: not all of those marriages had a major emotional impact on her.

LENGTH AND DEPTH

As you would expect, the longer and deeper the line, the more important the relationship. Sometimes the lines are so long that they are visible on the front of the hand as well as the side, in which case you can be sure this is a very important relationship. When the lines are faint, they indicate relationships that are important at the time of the reading, but whose impact may fade over the years.

THE FORMATION OF THE LINES

Look at each line to see whether it offers any clues about the relationship. If one line runs into another, it shows that one important relationship ended just before the next one started and sometimes that they were being conducted at the same time.

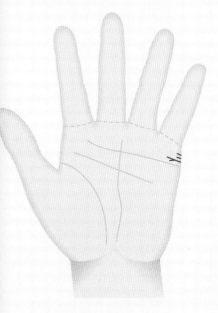

A forked line of marriage can show two relationships going on at once.

Expert tip

Is there a difference between the lines of marriage on the dominant and nondominant hands? The lines that appear on the dominant hand describe events that are fairly likely to happen, whereas the lines on the nondominant hand describe possible events.

RANDOM MARKS

As well as the major and minor lines, most palms are decorated with many different random markings. The ones we are going to discuss here are the star, triangle, cross, grill, square, island and chain. Each has a particular meaning, as you will discover.

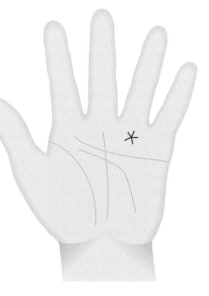

A star is only favorable when it appears on the mount of Apollo. In this position it denotes artistic success.

STAR

Make sure you are looking at a star and not a cross. A star always has more legs than a cross, so it must have at least five legs to qualify. A star indicates a shock or severe difficulty experienced in the area of life ruled by the part of the hand on which the star is found. For instance, a star on the mount of Jupiter shows a shock connected with the ambitions; on the mount of Saturn it indicates a shock connected with a responsibility or duty. There is only

one exception to the rule that the star is unfortunate: A star on the mount of Apollo indicates success in a career connected with the arts.

TRIANGLE

Take your time when looking in the
palm for triangles, whether large or
small. Once you start to search for
them, you will find that many are
formed by major and minor lines
intersecting one another, such as a
triangle created when the fate, head
and Apollo lines meet in the plain of
Mars. Focus solely on the triangles
that are very clearly formed by strong
lines, and ignore anything that is
vague, blurred or indistinct.

Triangles on the palm show skill
and training, especially if they are
connected to the head line. This
training will invariably involve some
form of technical ability. For instance,
you would expect to find triangles on
the palm of a doctor, engineer or
architect, who undergoes a long period
of training. Triangles will also appear
on the hand of someone who enjoys
learning new skills in his spare time,
such as car maintenance.

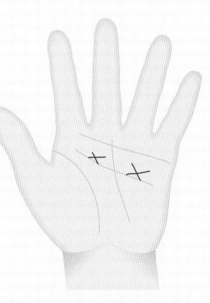

*These two triangles are formed by small
lines connecting with the head line.*

CROSS

As you might imagine, a cross
indicates problems. Think of it as a
crossroads, at which the person must
stop and decide what to do next. A
cross can be formed when a small line

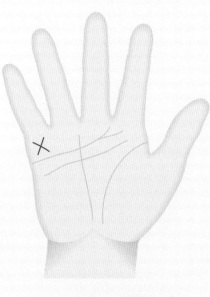

A cross on the mount of Mercury shows communication problems with others.

crosses a major one, or it might manifest apparently at random when two tiny lines bisect each other.

A cross represents obstacles that must be overcome, and difficulties that can lead to a change in someone's circumstances. The nature of the problem is shown by the position of

the cross on the hand—a cross on the mount of Venus denotes problems with relationships.

However, if a cross appears in the space between the head and heart lines, it has a different meaning. This is called *La Croix Mystique* and shows that the person is drawn toward the occult and mysticism. If the cross is close to the mount of Jupiter, he is interested in having readings in astrology, tarot and similar subjects, but does not want to practice them. If the cross touches the fate line, or the fate line forms part of the cross, his life will be strongly influenced by mystical and occult topics.

GRILL

A network of horizontal and vertical lines is another indicator of trouble. It usually appears on the mounts, where it shows problems connected with the meaning of that mount. For example, a grill on the mount of Saturn indicates a tendency to be depressed, to take life too seriously or to worry about work. The good news is that grills usually indicate temporary problems, and once these are resolved the grills will disappear. They therefore act as early-warning systems, telling you that some area in your life is about to become stressful.

SQUARE

Whether it surrounds a break in a line or appears on a mount, a square is a protective mark, helping to counteract

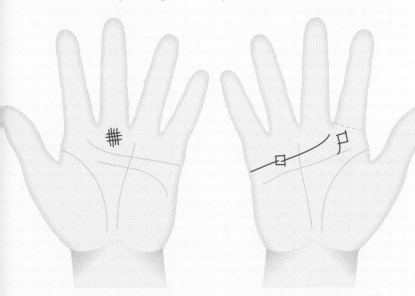

A grill on the mount of Saturn indicates a tendency to take life too seriously.

The teacher's square on the mount of Jupiter shows natural teaching ability.

any negative influences. For instance, a square on the mount of Jupiter helps to guard against conceit and over-optimism, and a square surrounding a break in the heart line helps to reduce problems in a relationship.

If you do find a square on the mount of Jupiter, examine it closely because it may be what is known in palmistry as a "teacher's square": one that is linked to the head line by a single line, so it looks rather like a flag. It shows that the person is a natural teacher because he is able to share his knowledge with others in an interesting and informative way.

ISLAND

An island can only appear on a line—never on its own. It looks like a tiny island that has interrupted the line, and in fact is the point where the line

ISLANDS AND CHAINS
a *An island on the heart line*
b *A chain on the fate line*

has divided in two before joining up again. It shows a weakness in the energy of the line, so if it appears on the life line it indicates a reduction in the person's health or vitality at the age indicated by its position. Unless the line is much weaker after the island, he will recover from the temporary weakness.

CHAIN

A chain is a collection of islands that appears on a line, one after the other. As you would imagine after having learned the meaning of a single island, a chained line shows a long period of weakness and lack of focus. That person's energies are not functioning properly and therefore the area of life ruled by the line starts to suffer. A section of chains on the heart line can sometimes indicate a period of illness, but this will always be confirmed by other markings on the palm. If you cannot find any, the chains show

Expert tip

When looking for random lines, always start from the same point, so that you get into the habit of working methodically. You could start at the mount of Venus and move over to the mount of the Moon, then the plain of Mars, and then examine the mounts underneath the fingers, or you might prefer to look at all this in reverse order.

instead that the person finds it difficult to express his emotions and form strong relationships.

BREAKS IN THE LINES

Traditional palmistry books are often full of dire predictions about the meanings of lines and various marks on the hand, making it a nerve-racking business to look at your palm because you dread to think what you might find. Many of these prognostications are unnecessarily doom-laden and negative. However, breaks in lines always indicate problem areas because they represent an interruption to the energy of that line.

BREAKS AND FREE WILL
Although we cannot do anything to change events that have already happened, we can certainly take steps to avoid future problems that are shown by breaks in the lines. So if there is a break in one of the lines on your palm, which predicts problems for the future, do not assume it is impossible to escape this event.

Forewarned is forearmed, and by taking avoiding action you may be able to reduce the forthcoming difficulty, even if you cannot completely escape it. Remember that lines on the hand can change, so do not be fatalistic about what you find in your palm. We tend to imagine that fate is something imposed on us by unseen forces, rather than the results of our own actions. But, as you will see from the palmistry case study further on (see page 245), this is not always true.

LOOKING FOR A BREAK
Examine the major lines on the palm carefully to see if any of them are broken. A broken line can be anything from a tiny gap that briefly separates a line to a massive breach, in which the two ends of the break stand far apart. If you do find a break

This is a big break in the life line and there are no connections between the two halves of the line.

in a line, you must assess its level of importance. This will tell you the amount of disruption that is caused by the event. Will it be a temporary inconvenience, as shown by a tiny gap, or a complete change of circumstance, as shown by a huge break? Using the timing techniques described later in this section (see pages 246–249), decide how old the person will be when the event in question takes place.

This break in the life line is surrounded by a protective square, which helps to reduce the problems that may be encountered.

PROTECTION

When you have found a break in the line, check to see whether it is protected by any other lines, because these will reduce its impact. If a square surrounds the break, it works like a patch covering a weak spot in an old pair of jeans, strengthening the line and counteracting the potential problems that may arise.

If there is no square, look carefully to see whether any small lines link the two halves of the line. You could think of these as tiny stitches that

A short sister line provides support for the break in this head line.

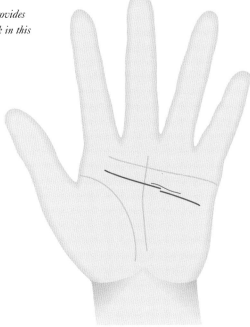

reconnect the energy of the two lines, so that although the relevant line is fractured, it is not completely disconnected. As a result, the event indicated by the break will feel like a minor blip or small setback rather than a massive disruption.

If you cannot find a small line linking the two halves of the line, see if there is a small sister line that runs beside the break. This will not touch the broken lines, but will act as a reinforcement and provide support during the event in question.

AFTER THE BREAK

It is now time to look at the condition of the line after the break, because this will tell you how well the person recovers from the event. If the line is stronger after the break, whatever is signified by that break will have a positive effect on her and the area of life ruled by that line will improve. For instance, if her heart line becomes stronger after a break, her relationships will get better. If the line is weaker after the break, she will be badly affected by what happens to her. A faint or chained heart line after a break shows that she will feel hurt and sad after the event in question.

Assessing the break

Ask yourself the following questions:

- *How big is the break?*
- *Is the break protected by a square or some other positive mark?*
- *What is the condition of the line after the break?*
- *Does the break appear on the same line on the other palm?*
- *Is that break protected by a positive mark?*
- *Are any other major lines broken at about the same age?*

ONE OR BOTH HANDS?

When you are satisfied that you have examined the broken line in as much detail as possible, look at the other palm to see if the break also appears on that hand. If it does, the event will have far greater impact on the person's life than if only one palm is affected. If it appears only on the dominant hand, she will have had no inkling of what was going to happen. If the break appears only on the nondominant hand, the event will affect her privately, but will have little outward impact.

CHECKING THE OTHER LINES

Examine the other lines on the hand to see if they also carry breaks at the age indicated by the first break. If they do, whatever is represented by that break will have a major impact on the person in the areas of life ruled by the lines.

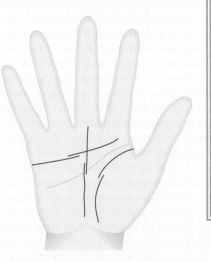

When several lines are broken at the same time of life, the predicted event will have a transformational impact on the person concerned.

Palmistry case study

The life lines on Jenny's right and left palms had large breaks joined by tiny lines. One night when she was driving home she fell asleep at the wheel of her car, but she was unhurt. Was this the event indicated by the breaks in her life line? No. A couple of years later she was sent to prison for embezzling a huge amount of money from her employers. That was the event shown by the breaks in her life line, and it was purely the result of her own actions. Jenny had created her own destiny.

TIMING EVENTS WITH THE LINES

When you start to read people's palms you will soon be asked to make predictions, and you will have to say how old you think the person will be when the predicted event takes place. After all, it is no good telling someone that he will have a major life change at some point within the next 30 years. He will want you to be much more specific than that!

MENTALLY DIVIDING THE LINE

The best way to time an event marked on a line is to divide that line in your imagination into equally spaced ten-year sections, with the start of the line representing the person's birth and the end of the line representing death. You can then gain a good idea of how old the person will be when the event in question takes place. For instance, if you are trying to time the event shown by a cross on the fate line, and it falls in the middle of the section from 40 to 50 years old, you can estimate that the person will be about 45 when the event takes place.

You must therefore know where each line begins and ends, otherwise you will be timing it from the wrong direction. Look at the diagram to refresh your memory, and remember that the head and life lines begin at or near the thumb, the heart line starts at the outer edge of the palm, while the fate line begins at the base of the hand. When timing the relationships shown by the lines of marriage on the outer edge of the palm, you work from the heart line up to the base of the Mercury finger.

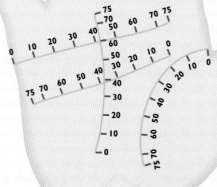

This diagram is based on an average life span of 75 years, but you will have to revise this if you are reading the palm of someone who is older than that.

When timing lines of marriage they run from the heart line up to the Mercury finger.

TIMING PREVIOUS EVENTS

If a major event has already taken place in someone's life, it will help you to check your timing for accuracy.

Work out how old he was at the time of the event and then ask him if your estimate is correct. This will enable you to do any fine-tuning that is necessary. This is especially useful when you are starting to read palms.

Cheiro (see page 11), one of the most celebrated palmists of the early 20th century, was able to predict not only the year, but also the month in which important events would take place. However, such accurate timing skills are beyond the reach of most of us, and he was undoubtedly using intuition in addition to his knowledge of palmistry. If you feel a similar urge to be specific about the timing of an event, it will be your intuition that is guiding you.

Expert tip

At the start of a session do not forget to ask the person whose hand you are reading how old he is. You need this information so that you can find his current age on each line of his hand. If you suspect he has given you the wrong information, remember that people invariably shave a few years off their age for vanity's sake!

PRACTICE MAKES PERFECT

It is best to practice on your own hand before trying to time the events shown on the hands of other people. Look carefully at the lines on your hand and see if you can find any breaks, islands or squares. Work out how old you were, and then consider what these marks might signify.

Alternatively, if you do not have many random marks on your hands, enlist the help of a cooperative friend who does have these marks. Ask him if you can examine his palm and if he will help you to interpret these marks and time them. You will learn a lot from this exercise.

LOVE AND RELATIONSHIPS

Love is a vital force of energy in our lives and we would be completely impoverished and lost without it. We all need some form of love to feel healthy and happy, although love comes in many forms. One person may feel the greatest love for her partner; another is wrapped up in her children; and someone else's world may revolve around her pets. People can also become completely devoted to a favorite activity or cause. With such an emphasis on love, no wonder palmists down the ages have been consulted by clients wanting to know whether they will meet the man or woman of their dreams, or asking whether a relationship will last.

Our hands show what sort of relationships we prefer, and how we behave in them. Are we faithful, flirtatious, heartless, romantic or idealistic? Will we have a happy life with our one true love, a succession of relationships, or would we prefer to remain fancy-free? Our hands have all the answers—if only we know how to read them.

RELATIONSHIP WATCHPOINTS

What should you look for in a hand when you want to assess the part that love will play in someone's life? There are two main areas to concentrate on: the shape and texture of the hand itself, and the arrangement of the lines on the palm.

Love is a very potent subject for most of us, but try to remain objective when examining someone's palm to find out how that person behaves in relationships. This is especially true if you have a vested interest in discovering this information, because it can be tempting to concentrate on positive indications and ignore negative ones.

You must also be wary of being judgmental about someone's emotional make-up, perhaps by being critical of him if your findings indicate that he is prone to infidelity or being undemonstrative.

THE SHAPE AND TEXTURE OF THE HAND

Always start your examination by looking at the shape and texture of someone's hand, because this will give you invaluable information about his basic personality. Here are some pointers to look for:

- Does he have a fire, earth, air or water hand?
- Is the texture of the skin rough or soft?
- Are his fingernails narrow or wide, short or long?
- Are there gaps between the base phalanges of the fingers?
- Is the mount of Venus well developed or thin?

Our hands reveal a tremendous amount of information about our attitude to relationships, both good and bad.

- Is the palm hard, springy or flabby?
- Does he have droplets on the backs of his top phalanges?
- Is the angle between the thumb and hand narrow or wide?

THE LINES ON THE PALM

When you have gained key information about the person by looking at the shape of his hand, you can move on to examining the lines on his palm. Here are some questions to bear in mind:

- Does he have a girdle of Venus?
- Where does the heart line end?
- Is the heart line curved or straight?
- Is the life line curved or straight?
- How many lines of marriage does he have?

HEART LINE

As you are looking at someone's palm to discover how he behaves in relationships, you will want to spend a great deal of time examining his heart line. You will already have checked to see where it ends, and whether it is curved or straight, to give you basic information about his emotional make-up, but now you must look at the heart line in more detail.

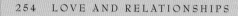

KEY POINTS
a *Medical stigmata*
b *Broken girdle of Venus*
c *Lines of marriage*
d *Lines rising from the heart line*
e *Fate line ending at heart line*
f *Forked head line*
g *Curved life line*

You must ask yourself the following questions:

- Where does the line sit between the top of the palm and the head line?
- What color is the line?
- Is it crossed by any lines of interference?
- Are there any lines of influence and, if so, are they above or below the line?
- Is the heart line broken and, if so, is it a serious break or is it protected by other lines?

OTHER CONSIDERATIONS

You should also consider other points about the person's hand that indicate his general attitude toward other people. For instance, is this someone whose main concern is for himself, or is he tuned in to the needs of others as well? Here are some things to look for:

- Is there a loop of humor?
- Is there a loop of seriousness?
- Are there any lines of children?

Important relationships, such as marriages, will be shown as marriage lines on the edge of the palm.

- Is there a ring of Solomon on the mount of Jupiter?
- Can you find the medical stigmata?

INDICATIONS OF LONG-TERM RELATIONSHIPS

Some people believe that love is for keeps and will do their utmost to make their relationship a success, staying with a partner even when things are at their worst. Others prefer to keep their options open, never committing themselves to a long-term partnership and disappearing at the first hint of trouble.

It is usually only experience that tells us whether the person we have fallen in love with will be able to maintain a relationship with us. Fortunately, palmistry can give us some answers a little sooner than that. So if you have fallen for someone, but are unsure whether she is a stayer or a leaver, here are some clues to look for in her hand. You could also examine your own hand to discover your own attitude to relationships.

THE SHAPE AND FEEL OF THE HAND

Start by looking at the shape of the hand. Ideally, it should be an earth hand, because this shows a practical, reliable and solid nature—this is not someone who is easily bored and enjoys romantic distractions. Instead, she likes familiarity and comfort, so she is temperamentally suited to long-term relationships and is prepared to work hard to make them successful.

Now check the feel of the person's hand. It should be fairly soft and springy, which shows that she is sensitive and understanding. This makes her more likely to consider her partner's feelings and show concern for them, and probably be interested in maintaining a healthy, balanced and satisfying relationship.

LINES OF MARRIAGE

These lines on the side of the palm (see pages 232–233), beneath the Mercury finger, show how many major relationships someone will have. She is more likely to be involved in long-term relationships if she has one, or maybe two, marriage lines that are strongly indented, because these show emotional

There are two strongly marked lines of marriage on this palm, indicating two very important relationships.

Some people have the ability to stay together for better or for worse.

connections that have touched her deeply. A collection of faint lines indicates a succession of relationships that she does not take so seriously.

HEART LINE

You will be paying a lot of attention to her heart line, because this shows how she expresses her emotions and what sort of relationships she is looking for. Someone who is interested in satisfying, long-term partnerships has a

Someone's heart line is an excellent indicator of how she behaves in relationships and what she gets from them.

heart line with a good, generous curve, preferably on both palms. The curve reveals her ability to show her feelings.

Look to see whether there are many small lines leading off the heart line. These are a good sign, because they show that she is capable of making emotional connections with other people, and therefore with her partner—something that is very necessary if you want to sustain a long-term relationship.

If a line leads from the heart line up to the mount of Apollo, it shows that she will enjoy a very satisfying and happy relationship. This is good news if the line appears on your own palm, and if it appears on your partner's you may hope that this line refers to you.

Where and how does the heart line end? If it runs across the mount of Jupiter and ends on the side of the hand, it shows someone who is very jealous, which could cause problems and heartache. However, if the line ends in a fan on the mount of Jupiter, it shows that the person has a delightfully affectionate and warm nature, and is therefore gifted at creating happy relationships.

Another favorable indication is when the heart line terminates in a

A heart line ending in a fork in these positions on the palm is a favorable sign.

fork, with one branch ending on the mount of Jupiter and the other between the Jupiter and Saturn fingers. This shows someone who is good-natured and fun and who puts others at ease; she is therefore less likely to encounter problems in her relationships.

INDICATIONS OF CHILDREN

Children are such a big part of someone's life that they will inevitably be shown on the palm. However, you must tread carefully when assessing what can be a very emotional and difficult subject for some people, especially if they desperately want children, but are afraid they will never have them. You must always remember that our palms show potential, which may not be realized for a number of reasons. So sometimes you will see children indicated on a palm even though the person in question will not have any.

It is also important to remember that the term "children" does not necessarily have the same meaning for everyone. For some people, a child means their flesh-and-blood offspring. Others may choose to remain childless,

but will be devoted uncles, aunts or godparents, or will become loving "parents" to their pets. Some people's "children" are their creative achievements, such as books, paintings or gardens. When these "children" are

Children, whether adopted or one's own, appear on the palm in the same way.

very important to the person, they will be shown in his hand. So do not be surprised if you see two children in someone's palm and the lines turn out to represent his cherished cats.

MOUNT OF VENUS

Before you look at the rest of the person's hand, examine his mount of Venus. Ideally it should be well rounded and springy, to show that he is loving and affectionate. Someone with a very flat mount is unlikely to want children because he does not have the emotional resources to care for them.

LINES OF CHILDREN

Look carefully at the person's lines of marriage. Can you see any fine, vertical lines that grow upward from the marriage lines, either touching the marriage lines or starting just above them? These represent the potential children that he will have. You may need a magnifying glass and a strong light to examine these lines accurately, especially if you are looking at a water hand that is covered with fine lines.

FROM THE OUTSIDE IN

You read the lines showing children from the edge of the palm inward, so the oldest child is shown on the outer

KEY POINTS
a *A thick line indicates a boy*
b *A thin line indicates a girl*

edge of the hand. This is a simple process if you are examining an earth hand with few markings, but is more complicated if this area of the palm is covered with vertical lines. If you find numerous lines, and they do not represent the person's children, they will indicate the pets, creative projects or other people's children that he loves.

The lines on our marriage lines describe the sex of our children.

BOYS AND GIRLS

When you have located the lines, the next step is to see which represent boys and which girls. Boys are indicated by long, wide lines; girls are shown by fainter, narrower lines.

FAVORITES

Look for any upright lines that either cut through the line of marriage or start from it. These represent the person's favorite child or children. For instance, if there are four children lines, but the final one runs straight through the line of marriage, it represents the child who is always thought of as the baby of the family and who gets special treatment as a result. However, even though this favoritism may be very apparent to you as the palmist, the person concerned may vigorously deny that he has a favorite child, because he feels guilty about it. As always, you must be tactful!

MULTIPLE BIRTHS

These are also shown on the palm. Twins appear as a two-pronged fork that rises up from the marriage line, while triplets are indicated by a three-pronged fork.

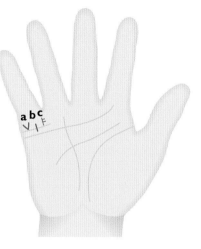

KEY POINTS
a *A thick fork indicates twin boys*
b *A thick line through the marriage line indicates a favorite boy*
c *Two horizontal lines indicate two grandchildren*

GRANDCHILDREN

You can also find grandchildren on someone's palm. These are marked as tiny lines that branch off the original upright lines of children, although you will definitely need a magnifying glass to see them properly.

THE FAITHFUL LOVER

Infidelity can cause a tremendous amount of heartache. Some people seem to be naturally unfaithful, liable to stray at any time, while others would never dream of betraying their partner. If you are currently involved with someone, which category does that person fall into? And, equally relevant, what does your hand say about your own ability to be faithful?

Remember that it is highly unlikely that anyone's hand will contain all the following characteristics. However, if you find three or more of the markings, these will suggest that the person in question does have a faithful nature. As you might imagine, the more markings you find, the more faithful she is.

THE SHAPE OF THE HAND

Look at the shape of the person's hand, because this will tell you about her basic personality traits. If someone is naturally faithful, she will have a practical, realistic earth hand. This shows that she is happy with routine, rather than always hankering for pastures new. The fingers should not be too flexible, because this shows impetuosity.

Check to see how much gap there is between the base phalanges of the fingers. Ideally there should be little or no gap, thereby showing that the person likes to keep what she has, rather than risk losing it.

Now look at the thumb. It should be fairly long, which shows a natural diplomacy and the ability to handle others well. Take a look at the fingernails, too. Someone who is faithful is likely to be fairly patient and tolerant, so look for spatulate fingertips with nails that are wide and of a normal length.

LIFE LINE

Look at the shape of the life line. It should be gently curved, indicating someone who has emotional warmth, but does not want to spread it around to all and sundry. Instead, she prefers relationships that are familiar.

Our hands reveal whether we are faithful or enjoy playing the field.

MOUNT OF VENUS

Now examine the shape and feel of the mount of Venus. The person is most likely to be faithful and loving if she has a mount of Venus that is nicely rounded without being over-developed, and which is nicely springy to the touch.

LINES OF MARRIAGE

Take a look at the lines of marriage on the outer edge of the palm. How many relationships can you see? This will give you some idea of how many serious involvements this person will have in her life, although you must bear in mind that harmless flirtations,

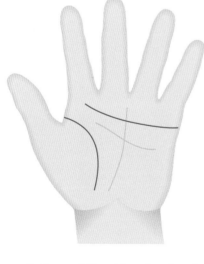

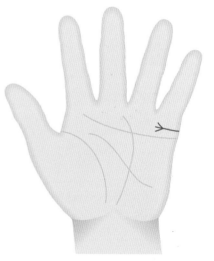

Gently curved life and heart lines show the ability to connect with others.

This three-pronged fork shows the relationship ended because of infidelity.

We do not all want the same things, such as stability, from our relationships.

wide range of emotions, because this is likely to increase her understanding of her partner, but not so long that it runs past the mount of Jupiter, because this shows a tendency to be jealous. Although a short heart line, ending on the mount of Saturn, indicates someone who wants her relationships to be successful, this person is also very passionate, which could sometimes tempt her into straying. So in a perfect world the heart line should end on the mount of Jupiter, which shows that the person is warm, affectionate and loyal.

Now look at the quality of the heart line. A very chained line shows a lot of emotional tension, which could come from infidelity. Small lines branching off from the heart line show the ability to make strong emotional connections with others.

one-night stands or brief affairs are unlikely to be shown here because they will not be important enough. However, such distractions will show up if they ruin a relationship, appearing as a three-pronged fork at the end of the line of marriage.

HEART LINE

How long is the heart line? It should be long enough to show that the person is capable of experiencing a

THE UNFAITHFUL LOVER

Sometimes the most surprising people turn out to be unfaithful. They may be loyal, honest and supportive of their partner while the relationship is going well, but look for distractions elsewhere at the first hint of trouble. Other people are pathologically unfaithful and find it virtually impossible to sustain a long-standing relationship, often through a fear of commitment.

Before examining someone's palm to find out whether he will be faithful, you must remember that all the marks indicate merely the possibility of infidelity, and not the certainty of it. You should also consider whether a tendency to be flirtatious automatically leads to emotional betrayal, especially

Look at the lines on someone's hand if you want to know his attitude to fidelity.

if your own hand shows signs of a
jealous nature.

THE SHAPE OF THE HAND

As always, you should start by looking
at the overall shape of the hand. If
someone is unfaithful, he is likely to
have a fire or water hand. Someone
with a fire hand is restless and easily
bored, so he may stray in order to keep
himself amused. Someone with a water
hand has a tendency to be romantic
and idealistic, and may switch from
partner to partner because he is looking
for his Princess Charming.

Are there spaces between the base
phalanges when this person's hand is
closed? If so, these spaces reveal an
open, friendly nature that means he
may get involved in emotional
entanglements.

MOUNT OF VENUS

How big is the mount of Venus? If it is
very full and bulbous, he is highly

*"What time do you call this?" Living with
a jealous partner can be hard work.*

sexed and passionate. This may, of course, lead to problems if he is tempted to stray by someone he finds attractive.

You can gain further indications of this by looking at the lines on the mount itself. Can you see rows of horizontal lines running across the mount? These are a sure sign of a flirtatious nature, although that in itself does not automatically mean the person will be unfaithful.

GIRDLE OF VENUS

The presence of a strong girdle of Venus is one of the classic signs that someone may be unfaithful. The more defined and clear the girdle is, especially if it appears on both palms, the more likely that person is to stray, because he is naturally flirtatious and attracted to others.

Look to see if any of the lines of marriage run into the girdle of Venus. If so, he wants to call the shots in the relationship, which may mean conducting it on his terms and expecting his partner to put up with his behavior come what may.

HEART LINE

By now you should be getting a good impression of whether this person is

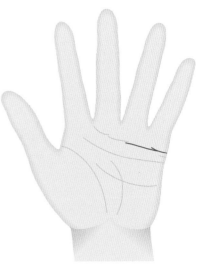

A girdle of Venus connecting with a line of marriage shows a need for control.

likely to be unfaithful. It is time to examine the heart line, which will show his attitude toward the people who love him. Is he heartless, selfish, inconsiderate or loving?

First, look at the shape of the heart line. If it is straight and strongly marked, this is someone who is very wrapped up in his own needs and desires, and who always puts himself first. The tendency is emphasized if the straight line appears on a fire hand.

You must now check the thickness of the heart line. If it is thin, it shows that he finds it difficult to love other people and is not very concerned about their happiness. He is therefore less likely to consider the effect of his behavior on his partner's feelings.

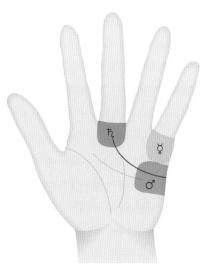

This person is cool but passionate, as shown by their very curved heart line.

Expert tip

The Mercury fingers will tell you a lot about someone's honesty. If the fingers are very bent, that person is good at telling tales. Such powers of invention may be extremely useful when it comes to finding good excuses for not being around.

THE ROMANTIC LOVER

Are you a romantic or a realist? Do you always see the best in other people, and do you forgive them even though they keep hurting you with the same behavior? Are you convinced that Mr. or Ms. Right is out there somewhere,

A born romantic has a tendency to view the world—and especially her beloved—through rose-colored glasses.

and that your whole life will change for the better when you finally meet this wonderful person?

Your hand holds the answers to all these questions, and may surprise you by revealing traits of which you are unaware. Of course, you can examine other people's hands to see if they are idealistic or whether they have both feet planted squarely on the ground.

THE SHAPE OF THE HAND

What shape is the hand? The true romantic invariably has a water hand, which reveals her sensitive nature and her tendency to be easily hurt. She is someone who is highly susceptible to the behavior of others, and who may find it hard to protect herself, because she is so open to outside influences.

People with fire hands can also be idealistic. They are so enthusiastic and imaginative that they always hope for the best, and have a tendency to trust to luck. Whereas the owner of a water hand may be crushed by unfortunate experiences, someone with a fire hand has a much better chance of bouncing back, ready for another skirmish with fate. You could describe this behavior as idealistic, because sometimes people with fire hands do not learn from their mistakes and continue to repeat them, each time vainly hoping that things will be different, but without taking any steps to ensure that they will.

THE SHAPE OF THE FINGERS

Now take a look at the shape of the fingers. The more pointed they are, the more romantic the person is. This tendency is even more pronounced if she has droplets on the backs of the top phalanges of her fingers, because these show immense sensitivity to her

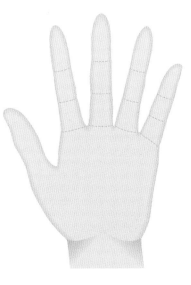

A water hand with pointed fingers and long top phalanges shows idealism.

surroundings and to other people. She is someone who is easily hurt. Long top phalanges of the fingers are another indication of a romantic and idealistic nature.

HEART LINE

You will want to look closely at this line, because it says so much about someone's emotional life and how she responds to others. Someone who has romantic ideals will have a heart line that is placed high on her palm, especially if she has a water or fire hand. Another important proviso is that the heart line should be generously curved, which reveals depth of feeling and the ability to connect with others.

Look to see where the heart line ends, because this will tell you a lot about the person's approach to relationships. A romantic idealist has a heart line that either ends high on the mount of Jupiter or runs up into the finger of Jupiter itself. A placing like this shows someone who instinctively puts loved ones on pedestals, believing that they are almost superhuman and incapable of

When two romantics get together they can spend much of their lives dreaming about how things could be.

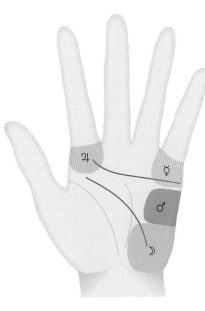

This heart line ends on the mount of Jupiter and the head line slopes steeply down to the mount of the Moon.

behaving badly. She is then very hurt and disappointed when, as inevitably happens, she discovers that the object of her affections has feet of clay after all. She may even feel betrayed.

HEAD LINE

When you have examined the heart line thoroughly, it is time to take a look at the head line, which shows the way someone thinks and will help to confirm whether her thoughts run along romantic lines.

You are looking for a curved head line, especially on both palms, as this shows that the person has a good level of imagination. Romantics are nothing if not imaginative, because they spend a lot of their time dreaming about how they would like things to be. If the head line is not only curved, but slopes down toward the mount of the Moon, this person's imagination is even more pronounced. However, she is prone to depression, so will become very miserable if her romantic reveries fail to come true.

A very straight head line shows someone who is a realist rather than an idealist. She believes romantic idealism is strictly for the birds.

THE PASSIONATE LOVER

When someone is passionate, he throws himself heart and soul into his relationships, as well as into every other area of his life. A passionate person often operates on the level of all or nothing, and needs complete involvement in whatever he is doing in order to feel satisfied.

Here, we are discussing what makes a passionate lover, but you could apply many of these rules to other passions in life, such as an activity or cause to which someone devotes all of his spare time.

THE SHAPE OF THE HAND

Which element does the person's hand belong to? Someone with a fire hand will have much more instinctive passion and enthusiasm than someone

with a water or air hand. The owner of an earth hand can also be passionate, provided that his heart line is nicely curved—his emotions are much cooler when the heart line is straight.

Hold the person's hand to discover what it feels like. Ideally it should be

The indications of sexual passion on a palm can apply to other passions as well.

soft without being flabby (which shows a lack of motivation), as this reveals a sensuous nature. It should also feel warm and responsive.

THE THUMB

Now examine the person's thumb. A long thumb reveals good reasoning ability, while a short thumb shows that he finds it hard to control his feelings and may therefore be swept away by emotion and passion.

MOUNT OF VENUS

Passion and a flat mount of Venus do not go together. The truly passionate person has a highly developed mount of Venus, which shows that he is ruled by a strong sex drive and powerful libido. The mount will be a good color and not too pale. He may also have a strongly marked line of Mars passing through the mount of Venus, indicating that he has a lot of physical stamina and vitality.

SIMIAN LINE

When someone's head and heart lines have been replaced by a simian line, it shows that he cannot distinguish between his thoughts and feelings. Although simian lines are relatively rare, they often appear on the hands of people who are very passionate and

Passion personified—an unbroken girdle of Venus and a simian line.

Is passion in the bedroom balanced by emotional rapport in everyday life?

sensual and who struggle to hide these characteristics. It is as though they lack one of the usual ways of controlling their personality, so tend to behave very impetuously.

GIRDLE OF VENUS

If someone is often carried away by his emotions, it is highly likely that at least one of his palms has a girdle of

Venus. The clearer this is, with few or no breaks, the more that person is ruled by his feelings. If the girdle has such a deep curve that it comes close to the heart line, or actually touches it, he finds it virtually impossible to put a brake on his turbulent and overwhelming emotions.

HEART LINE

As we are dealing with matters of the heart, you cannot ignore the heart line. If the person has a simian line on only

Low-set heart and head lines show someone who is governed by his emotions.

Mars in the center of the palm. This shows someone who is completely at ease with expressing his feelings physically through sex.

The tendency is increased if the heart line either ends at the top of the mount of Saturn or climbs past this to the finger of Saturn itself, indicating someone who is extremely sensual and highly sexed.

one hand, pay particular attention to the heart line on the other hand.

First of all, consider the curve of the heart line. The rule is that the deeper the curve, the more passionate the person is. Here, you are looking for a heart line that curves so deeply downward that it enters the plain of

Expert tip

Sometimes passion leads to jealousy and possessiveness. When the heart line is very long, running right across the palm and ending on the side of the hand, underneath the finger of Jupiter, it denotes someone who is naturally jealous. Jealousy is also shown when both the heart and head lines are set much lower on the palm than normal.

THE UNDEMONSTRATIVE LOVER

Some people have no difficulty in showing their feelings, while others struggle to be demonstrative because they are simply not made that way. They prefer handshakes to hugs when meeting friends or family, and frustrate partners through their inability to be openly affectionate and loving.

Someone's hand will reveal whether she is demonstrative or emotionally reticent. Adults who are undemonstrative may find it almost impossible to change, but a child can be gently encouraged to become more loving and affectionate, and this alteration in personality will be reflected in the changes that take place in the palms. An inability to express emotion openly may be caused by fear of losing control.

THE SHAPE OF THE HAND

When someone finds it hard to show her feelings, she will almost inevitably have an air hand, with a square palm and long fingers. This person spends more time operating from her head than her heart, and likes to analyze situations from a logical perspective rather than get involved on an emotional level. The very idea of having to engage with her feelings will unnerve her. Someone with an earth hand will also sometimes be matter-of-fact and practical, to the point of thinking that demonstrations of emotion are silly or a waste of time.

Look at the angle between the thumb and the edge of the hand. A narrow angle, especially if present on both hands, shows a lack of emotional generosity and spontaneity.

THE TEXTURE OF
THE SKIN

It can be difficult to judge the feelings of someone who is undemonstrative.

Is the skin rough or smooth? Someone with smooth skin will always be more openly affectionate than someone with rough skin, no matter how her hand is shaped. You must also check the firmness of the palm, as a hard palm indicates an unemotional nature and a rather brusque way of relating to others. A very soft palm, which feels flabby, shows someone who lacks motivation and may therefore be undemonstrative, because she cannot summon up the necessary energy to show her feelings.

This woman has crossed her arms over her chest in a defensive posture.

MOUNT OF VENUS

The mount of Venus describes the ability to give and receive love, so a flat mount shows someone who finds it hard to show her feelings and who places little importance on the emotional side of life. The tendency will be reinforced if the life line stays close to the mount of Venus, indicating someone who is reluctant to stray too far from familiar people and situations.

HEART LINE

The curvature of the heart line will give you more information about someone's emotional warmth. Essentially the straighter the line is, the less demonstrative that person is. A very straight heart line therefore shows someone who is emotionally distant and closed off from others.

This tendency is increased if the heart line ends on the mount of Saturn. Not only does this make the heart line short, thereby showing that the person will never experience the range of emotions open to someone with a long heart line, but it shows that she responds better to sex than to straightforward love.

A heart line high on the palm, near the base of the fingers, indicates someone who is friendly, but more analytical than emotional.

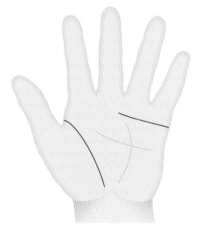

This short, straight heart line is compounded by an almost straight life line.

FAMILY RING

The family ring is a minor line that marks the point where the middle phalange of the thumb joins the palm. Its clarity and depth will tell you a lot about someone's feelings for her family. If the ring is weak and faint, she has little family feeling and barely any interest in maintaining blood ties.

KEY POINTS
a *Ring of Saturn under the Saturn finger*
b *Weak and broken family line*

RING OF SATURN

This is another minor line. It is a curved line that sits on the mount of Saturn beneath the base of the Saturn finger—do not get it confused with the crease mark where the finger joins the palm. The ring of Saturn shows someone who prefers her own company, finds it hard to relate to others and dislikes social activities.

AMBITION AND CAREER

Some of us are born leaders; others are entrepreneurs. Some seem to court success no matter what they do; others gain satisfaction from working hard all their lives, even if they never actually make it to the top. Most of us have to cope with the inevitable ups and downs of life along the way.

All these tendencies are shown in our palms, if only we know how to read them. This section describes some of the types of people who succeed in their careers, so that you can look for these indications in your own palms and decide how best to use them. Have you always secretly wanted to be an entrepreneur with enough faith in your own ideas to put them into practice and make money out of them? Do you see yourself as a successful leader who sets examples that others can follow? You will be able to find out whether you have the necessary skills and personality, purely by looking at your hands.

AMBITION WATCHPOINTS

When you are examining someone's hands for indications of how he will fare in his career, and whether or not he is ambitious and hard-working, you must remain objective and try not to let your own opinions color your judgments. For instance, you might have an instinctive antipathy toward this person's attitude, such as wanting to make a lot of money or have a great deal of power, but you must put this to one side when examining his hand. Think of it as an exercise in detective work: can you see the relevant features in his hand? The more features you find that correspond with his hopes, the more likely he is to attain his ambitions.

After you have examined the basic shape of the person's hand you need to concentrate on particular areas of the palm.

This man has a solid, practical hand with fleshy base phalanges to his fingers.

KEY POINTS
- **a** *Square fingertips*
- **b** *Long Jupiter finger*
- **c** *Strong fate line starting at the mount of the Moon with the line of Apollo rising from it at the head line*

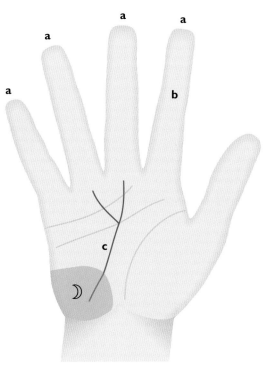

JUPITER AND SATURN FINGERS

These are two of the most important areas of the hand when you are studying someone's ambitions. The Jupiter finger describes leadership potential. It also shows whether he is able to tread his own independent path through life or prefers to follow in other people's footsteps. The Saturn finger describes his sense of responsibility and attitude toward his career. Here are some guidelines to help you get started:

- Is each finger long or short?
- Does the Jupiter finger jut out from the rest of the palm?
- What shape is each fingernail?
- What are the fingerprint patterns?
- Does the person wear a ring on either of these fingers?
- Are the mounts well developed?
- Is there a gap between the Jupiter and Saturn fingers?

THE THUMB

Never underestimate the power of the thumb, because it has so much to say about will power and strength of character. Someone with a weak thumb will always struggle to assert himself or make his mark in the world, even if the other indications on his hand are much more positive.

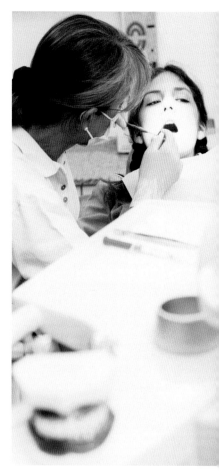

Some professions need a long training. Can the person see it through?

Here are some points to consider:

- How strong is the thumb?
- What is the fingerprint pattern?
- Is one phalange longer than the other?
- Is the top phalange thick or thin?
- Is it flexible or stiff?
- How big is the angle between the thumb and the hand?

HEAD LINE

The head line shows someone's reasoning ability and the way he thinks. It also shows his level of imagination, which can fire him with new ideas or give him a tendency to worry. Check the following:

- Does the head line start on the mount of Jupiter?
- Is the head line straight?
- Does it run down toward the mount of the Moon?
- Is it crossed by worry lines?
- Is there a simian line instead of a head line on either of the palms?

FATE LINE

This is the line that describes someone's path through life and is the one most closely connected with career. Ask yourself these questions:

- Where does the fate line start?
- Does it run free of the life line?
- Is it clear or fragmented?

OTHER CONSIDERATIONS

Here are some other points to look for:

- Is there a loop of seriousness on one or both palms?
- How strong is the line of Apollo?
- Does the line of Apollo rise from the head line?
- What is the predominant fingerprint pattern?
- Does the Mercury finger show good communication skills?

THE ENTREPRENEUR

Think of someone who is an entrepreneur, such as Henry T. Ford or Richard Branson. Consider the personal qualities that have given them the impetus and drive to succeed, because these are what you will be looking for in the hand. Entrepreneurs have faith in their own abilities and the determination to pursue their ideas until they become reality. What might be stumbling blocks for most people become challenges for entrepreneurs, who enjoy finding their way around problems and coming up with best-selling solutions.

THE SHAPE AND FEEL OF THE HAND
People with water hands rarely become entrepreneurs because they do not have the emotional resilience to make their way in such a cut-throat world. People with fire hands, however, have the enthusiasm and innovative spirit that is an important part of being an entrepreneur. What is more, they have the courage to take risks, time and again.

Now look at the fingertips. Ideally the majority of the fingertips on the hand should be spatulate, because these complement many of the positive, pioneering qualities of the fire hand. It may help to have one or two square fingertips, which will show a liking for practicality.

How does the palm feel? It should be springy and firm to the touch, but certainly not hard, to show that the person has plenty of energy and motivation.

THE FINGERS
Are there any gaps between the bottoms of the fingers? A gap between

An entrepreneur needs self-confidence and the ability to rise above setbacks.

the bases of the Jupiter and Saturn fingers is an encouraging sign, because it shows someone who is independent and happy to go her own way in life.

Now study the Jupiter finger. Is it long and strongly formed, indicating powers of leadership? If it sticks out from the rest of her hand, it indicates someone who has no qualms about asserting herself and standing out from the crowd.

The ability to take risks is shown by a long finger of Apollo. An entrepreneur also needs to be able to communicate ideas to others, so the

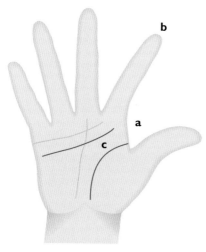

KEY POINTS

a *A wide angle between the thumb and hand*

b *Jutting Jupiter finger*

c *Space between the start of the head and life lines*

Mercury finger should be long and well formed. An entrepreneur requires good business sense, too, which is shown by a long base phalange on the Mercury finger. If it curves gently toward the Apollo finger, the person is shrewd.

THE THUMB

This should be long, wide and strong, to show character and the resilience to bounce back from setbacks. How flexible is it? Entrepreneurs need to adapt to changing circumstances without losing sight of their goals, so the top phalange of the thumb should be slightly flexible. How big is the angle between the thumb and the side of the hand? The bigger the angle, the more adventurous that person is. If the angle is greater than 90 degrees, she has a powerful need to go her own way and will risk anything to make this happen.

HEAD LINE

An entrepreneur needs a good brain, so you must look closely at the head line. It should be well formed, with a space between the start of the head and life lines to show independence and the ability to stand on one's own two feet. If the end of the head line

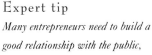

moves toward the mount of the Moon, without diving straight into it, this person has a good imagination.

Entrepreneurs must have plenty of successful and original ideas, which are shown when the line of Apollo is clearly marked and rises from the head line toward the mount of Apollo.

Expert tip
Many entrepreneurs need to build a good relationship with the public, whether directly or through publicity-seeking appearances. This ability is shown on the hand when the fate line rises from the mount of the Moon.

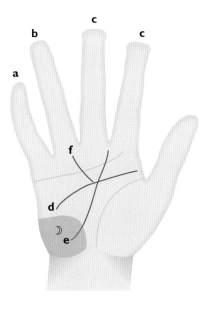

KEY POINTS
a *Long Mercury finger curving toward the Apollo finger*
b *Long Apollo finger with square tip*
c *Jupiter and Saturn fingers with spatulate tips*
d *Curved head line moving toward the mount of the Moon*
e *Fate line starting on the mount of the Moon*
f *Line of Apollo rising just above the head line*

THE HARD WORKER

Are you a hard worker? Are you even a workaholic, or does your idea of heaven run along very different lines? You probably already know the answers to these questions, but you may not be so sure when it comes to assessing whether colleagues and employees are industrious. Time will always tell, of course, but this could be an expensive or frustrating experience if you discover that you are left doing all the work while everyone else takes it easy. However, palmistry can give you all the information you need, provided you know what to look for.

Many of the characteristics described here can be determined by careful observation of someone's hand without having to read it in detail. This means that you can read a person's hand, without appearing to, when you are interviewing him for a job or considering whether to work with him.

THE SHAPE OF THE HAND

The hand's shape is always important, but it is particularly informative when you want to assess someone's sense of responsibility and industriousness. An

Someone who is industrious channels most of his energy into his work.

Hard work can involve manual labor but mental tasks can also be tiring.

earth hand shows that the person is practical and has ability. He is capable of achieving sustained sessions of hard work, and will still be plodding on in determined fashion long after someone with a fire or water hand has given up and gone home. The owner of an earth hand takes things slowly but surely, so do not expect him to work at lightning speed because this is not in his nature. Nevertheless, he is both methodical and trustworthy.

THE FINGERS

How does the person hold his hand when it is relaxed? Ideally he should keep his fingers close together, which shows that he is careful and does not like taking risks. These tendencies are confirmed if the base phalanges of the fingers are thick and there are no spaces between them.

Are the joints of the fingers knotty or smooth? If they are knotty, the person likes to analyze situations and mull them over until he is satisfied with his answers. Smooth fingers, however, show someone who makes decisions based on instinct and intuition, and who is therefore happier in a fast-paced working environment.

THE FINGERTIPS

How are the fingertips shaped? If there are more square fingertips than any other shape, the person is very practical, patient and likes to lead an ordered life. He loves structure and organization, so this is the ideal candidate for running an office or managing a filing system.

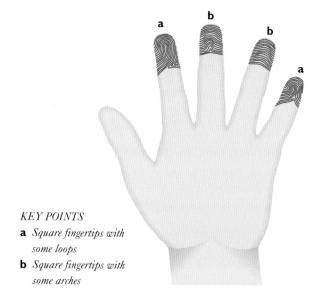

KEY POINTS
a *Square fingertips with some loops*
b *Square fingertips with some arches*

JUPITER FINGER

You are looking for signs that the person is well organized and confident, so the Jupiter finger should be strong and well formed. If this person will be taking orders from others, his Jupiter finger should not be too long or too prominent, otherwise he will struggle to accept anyone else's authority.

SATURN FINGER

This is the finger that shows whether someone has a sense of responsibility. If he has, his Saturn finger is long and well developed. If it dominates every other finger, he tends to make heavy weather of problems.

THE FINGERPRINTS

If you are able to examine someone's fingerprints you will gain valuable information about him. A majority of loops on the fingers shows that he has a liking for routine and is good at getting along with others, but may lack

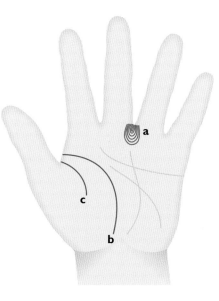

KEY POINTS
a *Loop of seriousness*
b *Curved life line*
c *Mars line*

the ability to take the lead. If there are more arches than any other pattern, this person is very practical and organized. He excels at working with his hands, but finds it hard to adapt to new situations.

THE BORN LEADER

You will find born leaders in every profession and every walk of life. They are politicians, captains of industry and office managers, but you will find many of them in less exalted positions as well. The natural leader is the person who always organizes the local summer fête, who spearheads a campaign against an unpopular government proposal, or who runs fund-raising activities for her favorite charities. She always has some project on the burner and, even though she may jokingly complain about being run ragged and never having a moment to herself, you know full well this is how she likes it. She would be

The hand of a born leader must show confidence and motivation.

lost without something or someone to organize, whether she is the head of a big company or runs a youth club in her spare time.

THE SHAPE AND FEEL OF THE HAND

When someone is a born leader, she is outgoing and has excellent powers of communication, so she is most likely to have either a fire or air hand. Someone with a fire hand has seemingly endless reserves of energy and enthusiasm, while the owner of an air hand excels at bringing people together and putting across her ideas.

A firm, elastic hand shows someone who is motivated, sociable and energetic; however, if the hand is too hard, she likes to get her own way even if she ends up hurting other people's feelings.

Overall, the hand should be strong and well developed, which shows energy and ability.

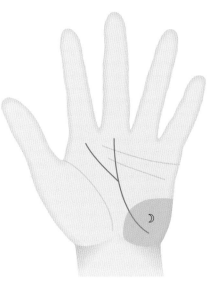

A fate line rising from the mount of the Moon shows determination early in life.

THE THUMB

You are looking for a strong thumb that is a good length. If the top phalange is very flexible, it shows someone who is adaptable and is not wedded to a particular way of doing things. Look at the thickness of the top phalange, because if it is very broad and bulbous

this person can be quite a bully when the mood takes her and will intimidate others into doing what she wants.

JUPITER FINGER

As the finger of leadership, this deserves special attention. It should be long and well shaped, showing someone who likes to take the lead rather than follow other people's instructions. If it juts out from the palm, almost as though it were stuck on at the last minute, it shows

The right clothes help to give a good impression and command respect.

someone who likes being in the limelight and enjoys the publicity that accompanies her activities. It may be difficult for others to work with her because this person is so keen to be the center of attention.

If there is a whorl on this fingertip, the person has a strong sense of individuality, which never fails her. This quality is accentuated if the

Look for a strong Jupiter finger and a good head line that starts beneath it.

MOUNT OF MARS

If you are going to take the lead you need courage, so carefully examine the mounts of Mars. A well-rounded mount below the Jupiter finger shows physical courage, which could be needed if this person is dealing with difficult situations or people. A well-developed mount under the Mercury finger indicates moral courage, which she will need if she is going to stand up for what she believes in.

Now examine the plain of Mars in the center of the palm. It should be firm, which shows self-confidence. If it is hard rather than firm, this person is very full of herself.

fingertip is spatulate, because she is prepared to take risks in order to get what she wants.

Study the mount of Jupiter. It should be rounded, showing ambition and drive, without being too large, which indicates an overwhelming desire to be in charge.

HEAD LINE

If someone is a natural leader, she needs the brains to get her message across to others, so the head line should be strong and clear. If it rises on the mount of Jupiter, she is good at putting her big ideas into practice.

SUCCESS AND ACHIEVEMENT

Not everyone has the same idea of success. For some, it means being in a position of great power, accumulating enormous wealth or becoming world-famous. Others have ambitions that are more modest by comparison, but which still involve being seen as a success by friends and contemporaries.

If you were to measure the sense of achievement that each person felt, would there be any difference between the person who is the head of a multinational company and the

The strength and quality of someone's handshake says a lot about him.

person who lands a good job in his local town? There is certainly little difference in terms of palmistry, as you will discover.

THE SHAPE OF THE PALM

This will tell you about the person's basic temperament and therefore in what area he can expect to be successful. Someone with an air hand will succeed in activities that involve communication, so he could do well in the media. The owner of a water hand needs to use his innate sensitivity, perhaps in an artistic capacity. Someone with a fire hand is looking for outlets for his dynamic energy and need to take risks, so might be good at sports. The person with an earth hand excels at practical activities and might make a successful farmer or gardener.

JUPITER FINGER

Pay close attention to this finger because it will tell you a great deal

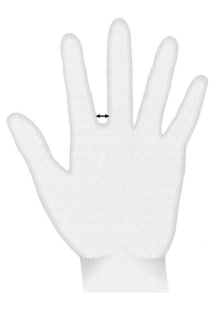

A gap between the Jupiter and Saturn fingers shows organizational skills.

about the person's drive and motivation. If the finger is long and well formed, he is ambitious and always likes to take the lead. He has a natural authority and does not like being told what to do, especially if he has a whorl on the Jupiter fingertip as

Someone who wants to be successful must be able to get along with others.

well. If he has a tented arch on the Jupiter fingertip instead, he will happily pursue his ambitions through thick and thin. An ordinary arch on this fingertip shows someone who wants to make the most of his practical nature. A loop here shows someone who excels at dealing with others. When there is a composite whorl, the person struggles to find his path through life because he is indecisive.

Is there a slight curve to the Jupiter finger? If so, it can show someone who eventually turns a hobby into a career, or at least manages to make some money out of it.

SATURN FINGER

Another important finger when assessing whether someone is going to be a success is the Saturn finger, which shows responsibility and business acumen. A long Saturn finger shows someone who will work very hard to get what he wants from life, especially if he can display his success through his possessions and high standard of living. This will be accentuated if he wears a ring on his Saturn finger, but no rings on any other finger. Someone with a short Saturn finger probably does not even have many ambitions, because he lacks motivation.

LOOP OF SERIOUSNESS

This marking between the Saturn and Apollo fingers does not always appear on the hand of someone who is keen to achieve his ambitions, but when it does it shows that he takes his goals very seriously indeed. He may even sacrifice other areas of his life in order to be successful.

> **Expert tip**
> *A simian line shows someone who is dedicated and very ambitious, and who will do his utmost to attain his goals in life.*

FATE LINE

If someone wants to be famous, he will be particularly interested in what this line tells him. If the fate line rises from the mount of the Moon and runs strongly up the palm, it shows someone who is in the public eye for some reason, perhaps because he is a household name.

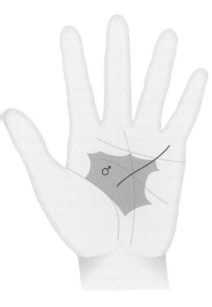

A sign of success in public life—the Apollo line starts in the plain of Mars.

UPS AND DOWNS

For most of us life is full of ups and downs. Although we may not like it when we are going through a difficult phase, learning to deal with this stressful time helps us to develop as people. We may also be more appreciative when our fortunes finally turn and start to improve.

Those who are trying to reach their goals are almost inevitably going to meet a few obstacles along the way. Here, you will learn how to find these stumbling blocks in the hand and

Most careers involve setbacks as well as successes, but how serious are they?

gauge their seriousness. This can be useful if you realize that your hand is indicating difficult times in the future, because you may be able to avoid them by taking a particular course of action now.

THE BASE OF THE FINGERS

Start by looking at the point where the fingers join the palm. Does this form a straight line across the palm or does it curve? When the Jupiter and Mercury fingers are both low-set on the palm, it shows that the person had a difficult start in life. She may have overcome this, but the memory will linger because it is shown so dramatically in her hand, and she may therefore be particularly worried whenever she faces a stressful or trying period.

FATE LINE

Look to see where the fate line starts on the palm. If it begins at some point above the wrist, it shows that this

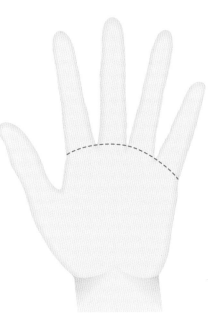

These Jupiter and Mercury fingers are both set low down on the palm.

person took time to find her feet and follow her chosen path through life. Now look at the rest of the fate line. Does it run confidently up the palm, getting stronger as it nears the fingers? If so, that person's direction in life will

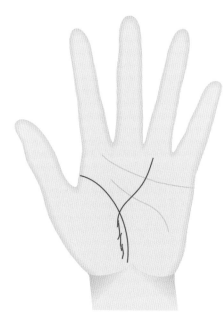

This fragmented fate line gets stronger after it moves away from the life line.

become more settled, assured and successful as she gets older. However, if the fate line is fragmented and weak throughout the palm, it shows that her life will always involve a lot of change and upheaval.

If the fate line begins tucked inside the life line, she will find it difficult to break free of her family's expectations and demands in early life. She will be expected to do what her family tells her, especially in terms of following a particular career, and will not break free of her family's all-pervading influence until the age at which the fate line crosses the life line and becomes independent of it.

HEAD LINE

When someone is facing difficulties, she will inevitably worry about them. These anxieties will be shown in the head line, so you must examine it carefully. Red patches on the line indicate a time of great anger. Tiny bars that cross the head line are worry lines, and the more deeply etched they are, the more serious the anxiety. Worry is also shown by a blurred patch on the head line, indicating a time of confusion and mental turmoil.

runs beside the broken line, which will provide some form of protection until the phase has passed. This might manifest as someone who helps the person through this bad patch. Alternatively, the break may be enclosed within a square, which shows that the impact of the change shown by the break will be lessened. Check the condition of the line after the break to see how quickly she recovers from her experiences.

These nails are short and broad, indicating a lack of patience and tolerance.

The person has a natural tendency to worry if the head line runs down to the mount of the Moon.

BREAKS IN THE LINES

Any break in a line indicates a difficult time that affects the area of life ruled by that line. Look for a sister line that

Expert tip

If you notice any grills, these show temporary problems connected with the part of the palm on which they appear. For instance, a grill that lies along the heart line shows difficulties in a relationship. The grill will disappear when the problems are resolved.

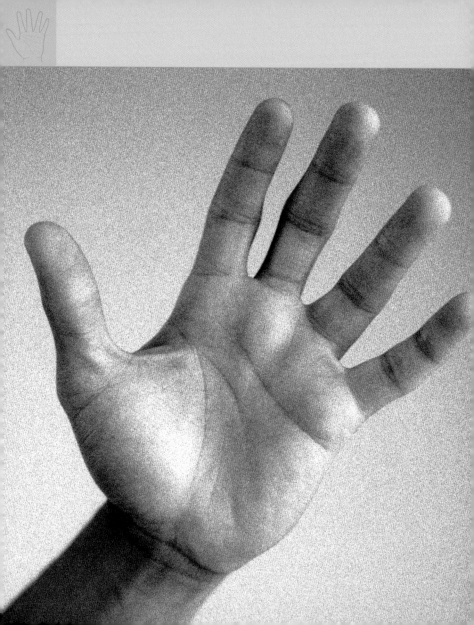

TALENTS AND ABILITIES

How do we make the most of our talents? Some people know what they are going to do in their life and follow that course unerringly; others are never quite sure and float from one interest or job to the next. The whole process can be as mystifying for the person who knew what he wanted to do at the age of seven as it is for the person who spends years searching for an activity or career that will satisfy him.

The answers are contained in our hands. Not only do they show our gifts and abilities, thereby telling us which direction to choose, but they also describe whether it will be easy or difficult to follow this path.

If you are already happily settled in your chosen career, you will be interested to see how your hand reflects this. If you are still searching, read the following pages to learn what your hand is telling you.

TALENT WATCHPOINTS

In this section we examine various vocations, such as writing, performing, healing and teaching, to see how they appear in the hand. Each of these vocations can lead on to a further range of career choices. In each case you need to think about the qualities and skills that are needed for that particular vocation, and then search for them in the hand. It will help to look at the hands of people who already practice these careers, whether you know them personally or see them on television. Study their hands for clues about what makes them successful in what they do, so that you can add to your palmistry knowledge.

As always, you must start by looking at the shape of the person's hand to discover which category it belongs to; this will tell you about her basic temperament. You must also examine the thumb in great detail,

When looking at someone's hand and assessing it for artistic potential, do not get carried away and exaggerate the strength of this person's talent.

because this gives you so much information about her strength of character. After this, you can study particular areas of the hand that you think are relevant.

APOLLO AND MERCURY FINGERS

Both of these fingers are important in the vocations described in this section of the book. The Apollo finger tells you about the person's artistic abilities, which she may choose to express in a variety of ways. The Mercury finger shows whether someone is able to communicate well with others, and the manner in which she expresses herself.

Here are some pointers:

- Is each finger long or short?
- What shape is each fingernail?
- What is each fingerprint pattern?
- Does the person wear a ring on either finger?

Most of us are gifted in some area of life, even if it will never win us an award or make us rich and famous.

- Are the mounts well developed?
- Is there a star on the mount of Apollo?
- Are there medical stigmata on the mount of Mercury?
- Is there a gap between the Mercury and Apollo fingers?

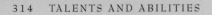

b

a

c

d

KEY POINTS
a *Curved heart line*
b *Ring of Solomon*
c *Medical stigmata*
d *Dipping head line*

LIFE LINE

The life line is very important when you are assessing someone's level of energy and general attitude to life. You must examine the mount of Venus, which is enclosed by the line, at the same time, because this will give you more information about her vitality and general level of energy. Here are some suggestions:

- Is the life line curved or straight?
- Is it a good color?
- Is the mount of Venus rounded or flat?
- Can you see any lines of Mars?

HEART LINE

This line tells you about the state of the person's emotions and whether she finds it easy to express her feelings. Many of the talents and abilities described in this section involve communicating deep emotions, so it is important that the person should be aware of her own feelings. Compassion and empathy may be essential, and these are shown by the curve and general character of the heart line. Consider these points when looking at this line:

- Where does the heart line end?
- Is it curved or straight?
- Does it have lines of influence running off it?
- Is it a good color?

OTHER CONSIDERATIONS

You need to consider these features as well:

- Does the head line end in a writer's fork?
- Does the head line run down to the mount of the Moon?
- Is there a ring of Solomon on the mount of Jupiter?
- Is there a teacher's square on the mount of Jupiter?
- Can you see the medical stigmata on the mount of Mercury?

THE WRITER

Popular belief holds that we are all capable of writing at least one book. But is that true? While some children start putting pen to paper almost as soon as they can read and continue like this for the rest of their lives, others are busy with different pursuits. Some adults blossom as accomplished writers quite late in their lives, while others talk of writing a book when they retire, but never get beyond the first few pages. As always, our hands tell the true story of our writing abilities. The ability to write comes in many forms, including fiction, non-fiction, academic texts and poetry, all of which appear in slightly different ways on the hand.

THE SHAPE OF THE HAND

You will find earth, fire, air and water hands in the writing profession, but, as you might expect, someone with an air hand will be especially good at communicating his ideas to his audience. Someone with a fire hand needs to write about subjects that fill him with intense enthusiasm, otherwise he will get bored quickly. Someone with an earth hand will be

Many people believe they could write a book but they need discipline and endurance in addition to talent.

happiest writing about practical subjects that deal with solid facts, while the owner of a water hand will want to write about topics that feed his powerful creative streak.

MERCURY FINGER

This is a very important finger for any writer because it rules the ability to communicate with others and express thoughts. Ideally it should be longer than average and strongly formed, but never clumsy or heavy. If it is knotty, the person likes to analyze situations and think about what he is going to write before he starts. If it is smooth, he relies on his intuition and gut instincts to tell him what to write. Check both hands to see if the two Mercury fingers look the same.

Many writers (especially if they are creative writers) consider themselves to be observers of human nature, so it is quite common to find a gap between the Apollo and Mercury fingers. It

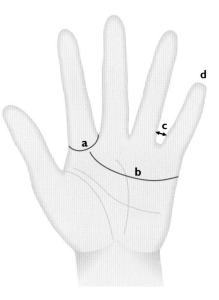

KEY POINTS
a *Ring of Solomon*
b *Curved heart line*
c *Gap between ring and Mercury finger*
d *Mercury finger with square tip*

shows that the person likes to hold a part of himself separate from everyone else, and is emphasized if he also keeps these two fingers apart when the hands are relaxed.

The shapes of someone's fingertips will describe the style of his writing.

Now look at the tip of the Mercury fingers. If each tip is pointed, it shows someone who relies on inspiration when he is writing, and whose ideas flow easily. If the tips are spatulate, the person likes to take risks in what he writes, perhaps stirring up controversy over his subject matter. Conic fingertips indicate that the person is drawn to artistic topics, and his writing will have an emotional quality. Square fingertips indicate someone who takes great care over what he writes, ensuring that it is clearly written and easy to understand. The process can take a long time, as the words may come slowly and he will continue to revise them until he is completely satisfied.

HEAD LINE

Another important indication of someone's ability to express ideas is the head line, so you must pay close attention to it. It should be long and clearly marked, to show that the person's mental processes are working well. A curved head line shows good powers of imagination, especially if it curls down to the mount of the Moon.

How does it end? If the person is a good writer of fiction, the head line should end in a writer's fork. This branch at the end of the head line shows someone's ability to see two sides to every argument, which is so important in creative writing, but is equally necessary for any writer who wants to compose interesting books that present a well-rounded idea.

This very clear head line ends in a writer's fork on the mount of the Moon.

THE ARTIST

Artistic talents come in many forms. Painters, illustrators, potters, sculptors, musicians and designers are all artists, so their hands will have some features in common. Performing artists, such as singers and dancers, have hands with slightly different characteristics that are dealt with next in this section (see pages 324–327).

Although it is tempting to imagine that all artists are sensitive souls slaving away in garrets for the sake of their art, successful artists of the 21st century need grit and determination if they want to succeed in what can be a very competitive market. You must therefore look for indications of ambition and staying power, as well as signs of artistic talent.

People who model their work with their hands, such as potters, are likely to have strong earth hands.

THE SHAPE AND FEEL OF THE HAND

You might imagine that most artists have water hands to indicate their sensitive natures. Although some artists do have this shape of hand, you will also find that many of them have fire hands, showing dynamic energy and endless enthusiasm for their work.

Whatever its shape, the hand should feel elastic and nicely springy. If it is very flabby, the person lacks the ability to motivate herself and may therefore give up at the first hurdle. Alternatively, this might be someone who always talks about her artistic plans but lacks the impetus to put them into action.

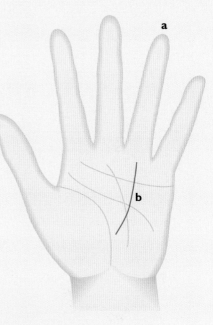

KEY POINTS
a *Long smooth Apollo finger*
b *Strong Apollo line*

THE FINGERPRINTS

Examine each fingertip to see which fingerprint pattern predominates in the hand and whether this matches the person's artistic ambitions. Someone with more loops than anything else is good at dealing with people, but has a tendency to conform to what others want, which would be a problem if she was hoping to become an innovative artist. A majority of whorl fingerprints indicates someone who delights in being an individualist, sailing against the tide if necessary. She may have a special talent that makes her stand out from the crowd. Arches belong to someone who is practical and skilled at using her hands, such as someone who makes jewelry or pottery.

APOLLO FINGER

A long, well-shaped Apollo finger indicates someone who is interested in the arts, but she needs much more than this if she is to turn her interest into a career. Study the fingerprint on this finger because it will give you many clues about her artistic abilities. A whorl on the Apollo finger, especially if it is present on both hands, is a very good sign because it shows that she has some form of artistic talent. An arch indicates that she could succeed at something that involves a sensuous expression of her artistic skills, such as sculpture or work

Look for a well-developed mount of Venus when someone works with a sensual and tactile medium such as wood.

with fabric. What is the shape of this finger? Ideally it should be pointed, to indicate that she has a strong sense of style and an innate artistic ability.

DROPLETS

Look at all the fingertips. Are they flat or do the majority of them have droplets? If they do have droplets, these indicate increased sensitivity and a love of beauty.

PERCUSSION

Now study the percussion on the outer edge of each palm. It should be curved to show artistic talent. If the curve is centrally placed, it shows someone who is able to put her creative ideas into action; if the curve lies closer to the mount of Mercury, it means that she may have lots of ideas that never see the light of day. When the curve is close to the mount of the Moon, her artistic inspiration is colored by a strong sense of practicality.

Expert tip

Can you find a whorl on the mount of the Moon? If so, it shows that this person has an excellent imagination that triggers many original and inspired ideas.

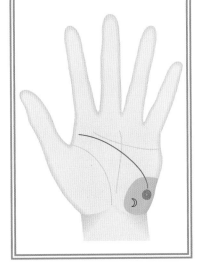

THE PERFORMER

What makes a good performer? Whenever you assess someone's hand to see if he is naturally equipped for a particular career, you must ask yourself what the qualities are that he needs and then try to find them in his hand.

There are many different performing arts, but the person who wants to succeed in one of them needs confidence, physical energy and the ability to communicate with his audience. In addition, dancers need bodily strength, actors need stamina and singers must be able to convey the emotional messages of words and music. They may also have resilient characters, as any performing artist will inevitably meet rejection and disappointment at times.

You may wish to extend the category of performer still further to include people who are involved in public speaking, and even salespeople who work by establishing an instant relationship with potential clients.

Do not assume that all performing artists are show-offs who love being in the limelight. Many of them are very shy.

THE SPREAD OF THE FINGERS

Watch to see how someone uses his hands when he is talking and how he holds them when he is relaxed. Does he bunch his fingers together or spread them apart? Widespread fingers indicate an extrovert nature, which can be very useful for some of the performing arts in which the performer has to engage fully with his audience. Bunched fingers could indicate someone who does not want to be the center of attention, such as a member of an orchestra or chorus.

This woman's fingers are held tightly together to soak up the applause.

THE ANGLES ON THE THUMB

The joints where the base of the thumb meets the wrist and at the bottom of the middle phalange will tell you about someone's sense of rhythm and timing respectively. These talents are essential for dancers, singers, musicians and acrobats, so it is important for these angles to be emphasized on both hands. Practice by looking at the hands of artists on television and in photographs.

APOLLO FINGER

This is an important finger for a performer because it reveals artistic abilities as well as the ability to connect with the public. Actors need long, well-developed Apollo fingers, as do public speakers. If someone wants to work with the public, he should ideally have spatulate tips to his Apollo fingers.

A star has an unfortunate meaning unless it appears on the mount of Apollo, in which case it promises great things, including success, artistic satisfaction and creative achievement. However, if the star appears only on the nondominant hand, the person will long for success but may never manage to achieve it.

MERCURY FINGER

All performers need to connect with their audience, whether through speech or mood, so you must examine the Mercury fingers to discover whether someone has good communication skills. The fingers should be long and well formed, especially if the person in question wants to write his own material.

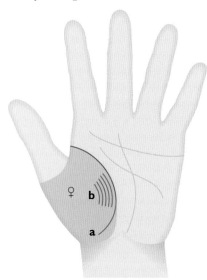

KEY POINTS
a *Curved life line*
b *Lots of small lines parallel to the life line on the mount of Venus*

FATE LINE

Will someone immediately find his niche as a performer, or will it take time for him to become established? The fate line will tell you. A strongly marked line of fate with no breaks shows someone who follows just one path through life, and the closer the line starts to the wrist, the earlier he discovered his chosen direction.

If the fate line starts independently of the life line on the mount of the Moon, it shows that this person needs to be in the limelight and will feel comfortable in the public eye, especially if these tendencies are confirmed elsewhere on the hand. If the fate line is reluctant to move away from the mount of the Moon into the center of the palm, he is a born performer, whether he is appearing on-stage or holding his friends spellbound with his latest anecdotes.

It is a rare performer who finds instant success and never loses it, and

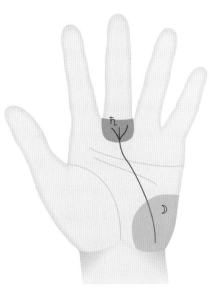

The trident on the Saturn mount shows three big ambitions achieved late in life.

most people need dedication and determination to survive hard times. If the fate line runs up to the mount of Saturn and then crosses over to the mount of Jupiter, it shows someone who will stick doggedly to his chosen path and never lose sight of his goals.

THE HEALER

"Healer" is a term that covers a wide range of disciplines, from conventional allopathic medicine to complementary therapies, and an equally varied

The shape of a healer's hand shows the type of healing she is drawn to.

selection of talents, from surgeon, nurse, family doctor, veterinary surgeon and dentist to osteopath, homeopath, acupuncturist, kinesiologist, and many more. A particular discipline or technique does not make a healer; instead, this

depends on a person's attitude and compassion toward others, and this is what you will be looking for in a hand.

You will not always find exactly what you are seeking, because people become healers for different reasons, including money, status, power and family pressure. However, all of these motives will be apparent in their hands, as you will discover.

Many doctors have enthusiastic fire hands, which help them to stay positive.

THE SHAPE OF THE HAND

The hand's shape depends on what sort of healing the person practices. Someone with water hands will be drawn to therapies that involve sensitivity, empathy and a gentle approach, such as crystal therapies, spiritual healing or color therapy. This person can rarely stomach the dirty, smelly and unpleasant tasks that are the lot of the hospital nurse, who is more likely to have practical earth or resilient fire hands. Most doctors have fire hands, enabling them to remain

enthusiastic and energized. People who specialize in talking cures, such as psychotherapy, tend to have air hands, which enable them to communicate with their patients.

MOUNT OF VENUS

A generously rounded mount of Venus indicates someone who is in touch with her feelings—a quality that is very important for healers. It also shows that she has vitality and stamina, which will enable her to top

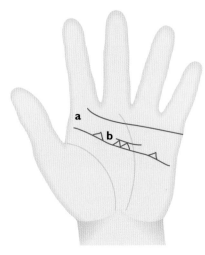

a *A wide gap between the heart and head lines*
b *Triangles on the head line*

up her energy levels when necessary. The life line should have a good curve, showing an outgoing, warm and friendly nature.

HEART LINE

If someone wants to dedicate her life to helping others, you will find evidence of this commitment in her heart line. The line should be nicely curved without being too extreme, and should end somewhere on the mount of Jupiter. Look for lines of influence running off the heart line, which will show emotional connections with others. There is probably also a wide gap between the head and heart lines, showing humor and openmindedness.

MEDICAL STIGMATA

You will find this small collection of lines under the finger of Mercury, but make sure you do not confuse the stigmata with the lines of children. If you do find the stigmata, they are a sure sign that this person has healing ability and has probably always been interested in medical matters. Even if she does not actively practice as a healer, she is the sort of person to whom others instinctively turn in times of trouble.

RING OF SOLOMON

It is highly likely that you will find this mark on one or both palms of a healer. It is a classic indication that someone is able to understand other people on a deep level and is interested in what makes them tick.

> ### Expert tip
> *If you see triangles on the palm, these little marks are signs of technical and specialist expertise. When you see them running along the head line, they indicate that the person will go through some form of training. In the case of a healer, this might involve anything from long years at medical school to a weekend first-aid course.*

This line of intuition runs from the mount of the Moon to the Mercury mount.

LINE OF INTUITION

Look for this curved line, which runs from the mount of the Moon toward the mount of Mercury. When it is present on one or both hands it shows that the person has a strong intuition, which can help her when healing others. In itself, it is not a sign of the ability to heal, but it can certainly assist someone in knowing how to treat a particular patient.

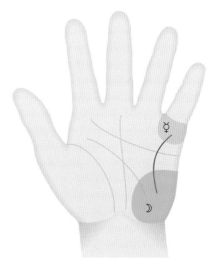

THE ATHLETE

When someone hopes to become an athlete, or devotes most of his spare time to physical exercise, you will see many signs of his sporting interest in his hands. However, at times you must do some lateral thinking in order to know what to look for. There is no special line to denote soccer prowess or swimming abilities, but you will be able to make intelligent deductions about someone's skills by studying various areas of his hands. Above all, you must look in the hands for evidence of physical vitality, drive, single-mindedness and endurance.

A soccer player needs plenty of stamina and is likely to have an earth hand.

THE SHAPE OF THE HAND

If someone wants to be a successful athlete, whether professionally or as an amateur, he needs energy, stamina and motivation. Someone with a firm, springy earth hand will have all three of these qualities, especially if he wants to pursue an aggressive and highly physical sport, such as boxing, wrestling, basketball or hockey. The owner of a fire hand is also well equipped for a sporting life, with plenty of dynamic energy and motivation. If the earth or fire hand is quite hard, it shows that the person is determined to do what he wants, even if it inconveniences everyone else. Such single-mindedness may cause family problems, but can be essential for an athlete who has to train every day, come what may.

KEY POINTS
a *Pronounced second joint of thumb*
b *Strong and long thumb*

THE THUMB AND FINGERS

These should be well shaped and strong. The thumb in particular should be long and with a good shape, to show plenty of energy and determination. After all, it takes great reserves of will power and motivation to jump out of a warm bed on a cold morning to begin pre-dawn training.

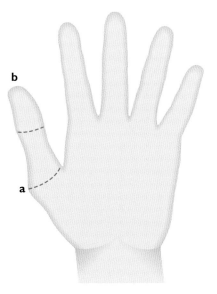

Sports such as tennis and basketball require a good sense of timing, which is shown by an emphasis on the joint at the bottom of the middle phalange of the thumb. This joint should be angular and prominent.

What shape are the fingertips? Ideally they should be spatulate, which shows that the person enjoys being energetic and needs plenty of fresh air. If the tips are square, he will take a very practical approach to his sport, which is likely to have a long tradition.

MOUNTS OF MARS

Someone may have plenty of energy, but does he have the courage that is needed for some sports? Start by looking at the inner mount of Mars nearest the thumb, to see how much physical courage that person has. A well-rounded mount of Mars shows a healthy amount of courage, but if it is too large he is full of bravado and can be foolhardy.

Timing is essential for a golfer, so look for the angle of timing on his thumb.

Now examine the outer mount of Mars on the percussion edge of the palm, which shows moral courage. If this mount is well developed, it shows that this person has the strength to resist temptations such as taking illegal performance-enhancing drugs, and has the guts to continue training when he encounters injuries and other setbacks.

LIFE LINE

This is another indication of physical vitality. Ideally the life line should be strong, well marked and a good color, with no large breaks or islands to show interruptions to the person's energy. It should curl around the mount of Venus in a generous curve, and the mount itself should be well padded, a healthy color and rounded.

Look inside the life line, near the thumb, for the line of Mars. When it is present and clearly marked, this is a further sign of physical strength. It is also an indication that the person needs to find healthy outlets for his high level of energy, so it is important for him to keep active.

THE SIMIAN LINE

A simian line, where the head and heart lines have fused into a single line, is always a sign of some sort of exceptional drive and ability, so when it appears on the hand of someone who is very sporty, it will increase his motivation and desire to win.

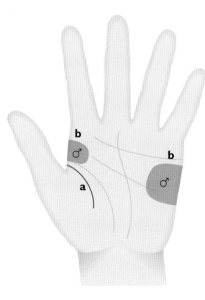

KEY POINTS
a *Strong line of Mars*
b *Good mounts of Mars*

THE TEACHER

Most of us have experienced the difference between being taught by someone who has chosen teaching because she did not know what else to do and someone who has an instinctive ability to convey her message with excitement and enthusiasm.

Don't be surprised if you read the palm of someone who is obviously a born teacher, but is following some other profession and denies all interest in teaching. She will inevitably find herself teaching sooner or later, whether it is actually in a classroom or giving informal talks in her spare time to local groups.

Are teachers born rather than made? Their hands would seem to say so.

THE SHAPE OF THE HAND

Above all, a teacher must be able to communicate her ideas and enthusiasms to her students.

An air hand will enable someone to convey her thoughts and words to her pupils, whereas a fire hand will manifest the sort of infectious enthusiasm and dynamism that entertains her students while teaching them at the same time.

MERCURY FINGER

This is an important finger because of what it says about someone's ability to communicate. It should be long and well formed, to help the person get her message across. If the finger is very long, or has a very thick top phalange, she is extremely talkative and may spend her classes chattering away about things that are not strictly relevant.

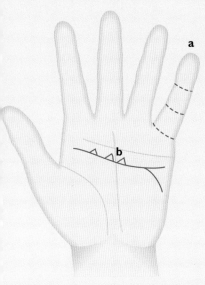

THE THUMB

If someone is hoping to take control of a class full of children or adolescents, it is essential that she has the necessary presence and self-confidence. Both these qualities will be lacking if she has a weak or short thumb, and she will struggle to keep control in the classroom. Ideally she should have a strong, long thumb with a waisted middle phalange, as this shows that she is tactful and good at handling people.

KEY POINTS
a *Long Mercury finger with thick top phalange*
b *Slightly curved head line with triangles on it, ending in a writer's fork*

HEAD LINE

Look carefully at the head line. It should be long, clearly marked and slightly curved, to show intelligence, imagination and intellectual sympathy

with others. If the line is short and very straight, this person cannot accept anyone else's viewpoint and lacks imagination. These traits are emphasized if the fingers and thumbs are stiff, and if there is only a narrow gap between the heart and head lines.

Does the head line end in a writer's fork? If so, this is good news because, in addition to writing ability, it shows

Teachers do not only work in classrooms. You will find them everywhere.

someone who is able to see more than one side to any question.

TEACHER'S SQUARE

This is a classic sign of natural teaching ability and you will find it on the mount of Jupiter. It is a small square joined to the head line by a little line. If it appears only on the nondominant hand, the person has probably considered becoming a teacher, but has never done anything about it.

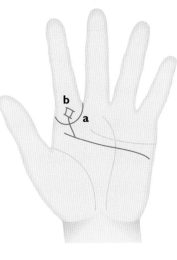

Palmistry case study

When she was a child, Carrie would line up her dolls in rows and pretend to be their teacher. As an adult, all thoughts of teaching vanished and she became a florist. Soon she was being asked to give demonstrations to groups of amateur flower arrangers and discovered that she loved teaching them. Sure enough, her hand revealed long Mercury fingers, teacher's squares and rings of Solomon on both palms.

KEY POINTS
a *Ring of Solomon*
b *Teacher's square attached to head line*

RING OF SOLOMON

The ring of Solomon does not indicate teaching ability, but it does show the important gift of being able to establish strong, sympathetic connections with other people. Such links are essential if a teacher wants to form an emotional and intellectual bond with her students.

TEMPERAMENTS

In this section we examine a wide variety of human temperaments, ranging from the spendthrift to the diplomat. This will give you further information about what makes someone tick. You will also learn more about yourself and your own motivations, some of which could come as a surprise. For instance, you might discover that you have a reckless streak, which you do your best to ignore, or that your strong yearning to travel the world is reflected by the marks in your hand.

Study the hands of your friends and family to see if they confirm your opinions about their personalities. You will probably find that each person belongs to several different categories, which will give you a good insight into how temperaments can overlap. It is also a useful exercise to look at the hands of people you meet only fleetingly, because even a glance will tell you something about their personalities.

TEMPERAMENT WATCHPOINTS

Human temperaments are so wide-ranging, and have so many idiosyncratic quirks, that no two people are alike. They may both display the same characteristics—such as being perpetually optimistic, or happiest when they are by themselves—but their motives and reasons may be very different. Even so, you can discover what sort of temperament someone has by looking at the general shape of his

A person's temperament is revealed in his hand if you know what to look for.

hand, plus the shape and color of his nails, even if you have only a few minutes in which to do so. This can be very helpful if you are hoping to gain an insight into the character of someone you are meeting for the first time, but who might play a significant role in your life, such as a prospective boss or partner. You may be relieved by what you see; equally you may be dismayed and decide that you do not want to take the relationship any further. You will also get a good idea of how to handle the person concerned, such as boosting their self-confidence.

The shape of someone's hand will always be a major facet of his personality, and it provides a bedrock of information on which you can build as you continue to examine the rest of the hand. The following suggestions will get you started, and you can then refer to the individual temperaments described on the following pages for more specific information.

Someone can try to disguise her bad temper, but it will show up in her hands.

THE FINGERS AND THUMBS

These give you valuable clues about someone's basic temperament. Unless the person is wearing gloves or is keeping his hands out of sight for some reason, you can gain plenty of information by discreetly observing his fingers and thumbs.

If you are able to examine his hands in detail, you can answer some

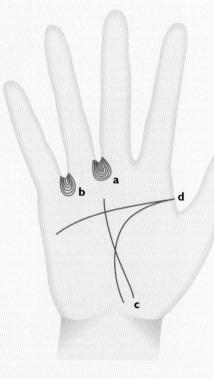

KEY POINTS

a *Loop of seriousness*

b *Loop of humor*

c *Fate line starting inside the life line*

d *Head line and life line joined at the start*

of the other questions posed here:

- What shape are the fingers?
- Are they knotty or smooth?
- What shape are the thumbs?
- Are they weak or strong?
- Are the thumbs waisted?
- Is the top phalange of the thumb thick and bulbous?
- How big is the angle between the thumb and the side of the hand?
- Are there any gaps between the base phalanges of the fingers?
- What is the predominant fingerprint pattern?
- What is the shape of the fingernails?
- What is the color of the nails?

HEART LINE

The heart line shows emotional responsiveness, giving you a good idea of whether someone is demonstrative or self-contained. Is he interested in other people, or is there only one person in the world as far as he is concerned?

Ask yourself the following questions when looking at the heart line:

- Is the line straight or curved?
- Where does it end?
- Do influence lines branch off the heart line?
- Is there a simian line instead of a heart line on one of the palms?

OTHER CONSIDERATIONS

Here are some other factors to consider. They will not always be strictly relevant, but they should give you more information about the person's basic character. Consider these points:

- Is there a ring of Solomon?
- Are the medical stigmata present?
- Is there a line of intuition?
- Is there *La Croix Mystique*?
- Is there a loop of seriousness?
- Is there a loop of humor?
- Is the Apollo line strong?
- Are there any chains, islands or breaks along any of the lines?

THE SPENDTHRIFT

For some people, holding on to their money is almost impossible. The moment they have any spare cash, they can feel it burning a hole in their pocket and have an overwhelming urge to spend it. Many of us have occasional phases like this when we go on an enjoyable spending spree, buying ourselves a few treats, but we usually do it in moderation and it does not become a major problem. If you fall into this category, your palm will display a few of the characteristics described here, but they will be complemented by markings that show financial prudence.

However, someone who is a real shopaholic will have many more of these characteristics in her hands. She might not even wait until she has the money, and might spend what she does not have, running up an overdraft or big debts on her credit cards.

If you are looking at the hand of someone who loves spending money, ask yourself why this should be. What is she compensating for?

Gaps between the base phalanges are a classic sign of being a spendthrift.

THE SHAPE OF THE HAND

This is an important indicator of someone's spending habits. A big spender is most likely to have a fire or water hand. Someone with a fire hand has a tendency to get carried away when out shopping, despite her good intentions. Someone with a water hand will distance herself from the harsh reality of how much money she is spending and simply will not think about it, in the hope that it will go away.

Look at the hand when it is relaxed. Someone who cannot keep hold of her money has large gaps at the base of her fingers. The fingers are flexible and most of them are smooth, which shows that this person is an impulsive shopper. All these traits will be emphasized if her fingertips are spatulate or pointed, both of which suggest that she acts on a whim.

What does the hand feel like? If it is very soft and floppy, this person lacks will power and motivation, so

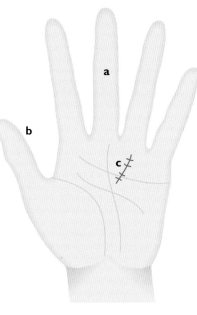

KEY POINTS
a *Water hand*
b *Short thin thumb*
c *Apollo line with small lines crossing it*

she will find it almost impossible to resist temptation. These tendencies will be compounded if the thumb is short and weak.

Some people have a neurotic compulsion to spend money, so look for signs of nervousness in the hand.

finger, which shows a lack of confidence. She may try to overcome this by wearing a flashy or big ring on her Jupiter finger.

If she is reckless with money and simply hopes that everything will sort itself out in the end, her Jupiter and Apollo fingers will be the same length.

MOUNT OF SATURN

Can you find this mount on the palm? It will not be present, or will be barely noticeable, if the person is highly irresponsible about money.

Another indication of a lack of responsibility about money is a short or weak Saturn finger. If it is very short, she is impulsive and does not really care about the outcome or impact of her actions.

JUPITER AND APOLLO FINGERS

These fingers will tell you more about someone's spending habits. If she likes to surround herself with status symbols in order to make herself look good, you can expect to see a short Jupiter

MOUNT OF VENUS

Does this person spend lots of money on beautiful objects or expensive status symbols? If so, you can expect the mount of Venus to be very full, which indicates an enjoyment of lovely things, although it can easily tip over into a love of ostentation and show.

LINE OF APOLLO

This line is connected with money, among other things. Look for small lines that hang down from the line of Apollo, because these indicate times when the person in question must be particularly careful with her finances. Small lines that run across the line of Apollo show obstacles in money matters that must be overcome.

Smooth joints show someone who is impulsive, especially if the Jupiter and Saturn fingertips are spatulate.

THE SAVER

Do you always spend your money or do you put some of it aside for a rainy day? It seems that people either have a natural instinct that makes them save their money or they do not: it can be very hard to switch from being an instinctive spender to being a committed saver because it involves a complete about-face about money.

If you want to discover whether someone is good at saving money, you must think about some of the reasons why he might want to do this. Does it make him feel safe to have some money stashed away for emergencies? Does he like to keep control of the purse strings? Does he like to put money aside for major purchases rather than get into debt? Is he scared that there will never be enough money for him, even when he is well off? Is he not so much a saver as a miser who begrudges parting with a single penny?

Someone who holds their thumb close to their hand is careful with money.

THE SHAPE OF THE HAND

Saving money comes easiest to the owner of an earth hand, because this person is instinctively practical and careful. He may also be a good gardener, giving him the satisfaction of saving money by growing his own vegetables and fruit. Equally, you are most likely to find square fingertips on the hand of a born saver, because they indicate caution and prudence.

Take a look at the hand when it is in a relaxed position. If the fingers are held closely together, the person is a good saver with a dislike of wasting resources. If he holds his thumb and index finger together when his hand is relaxed, he is extremely careful with money and may use it as a way of controlling others. For instance, this could be the parent who makes his children earn their pocket money, or the husband who never gives his wife enough housekeeping money. If he holds his thumb close to the side of his hand, this is another indication that he is careful with money. The smaller the angle between the thumb and hand, the less generous he is.

THE FINGERS

What do the base phalanges of the fingers look like? If the person is materialistic, they will be thick, with no gaps between them, and may also be the longest section of the fingers.

If a child is a natural saver he will start the habit at an early age.

KEY POINTS
a *Strong Apollo line with*
    small lines rising from it
b *Loop of seriousness*

Knotty joints are also a sign of someone who saves money, because they show that the person likes to analyze and think things through before taking action. Therefore he is unlikely to make expensive impulse buys without spending at least a small amount of time deciding whether he should do such a thing.

LOOP OF SERIOUSNESS

If someone is really committed to making the most of his money and putting plenty of it aside for the future, you will probably find a loop of seriousness between the Saturn and Apollo fingers. As the loop's name suggests, this person takes financial matters very seriously.

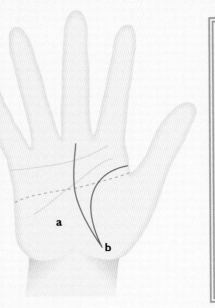

Expert tip

The minor Apollo line has strong connections with money and success, so it can tell you about someone's attitude to his finances. If the line is strong and clearly marked it shows success in life, which may well include financial prosperity. You would expect to see a strong Apollo line on the hand of someone who is wealthy, even if he prefers to save his money rather than spend it.

KEY POINTS

a *Hand with a big heavy base*
b *Life line with lines most strongly marked at the base of the hand*

THE THREE WORLDS

If you divide the person's hand up into the three worlds (see pages 62–63), which section is the largest? If he is primarily concerned with financial security, it will be the lowest section, from the thumb downward, which rules the material world. If this part of the hand looks very heavy or the lines are strongest here, he may be very materialistic, especially if he also has thick base phalanges to his Saturn and Apollo fingers.

THE ETERNAL OPTIMIST

Optimism is not only a state of mind, it is a way of life. Optimists have an inbuilt resilience that helps them to bounce back from setbacks, and an innate faith that reassures them that everything will work out well. Of course, there is a difference between optimism and wishful thinking, but here we are concentrating on positive thinking and the ability to find a silver lining in even the darkest cloud. Can such attitudes be seen on the hand? They can, if you look for all the ideas and beliefs that constitute an optimist.

THE SHAPE OF THE HAND

Most optimists have fire hands, because this is the shape that indicates a seemingly endless enthusiasm for life. The owner of a fire hand has plenty of emotional and physical energy, which helps her to cope with life's ups and downs, as well as having lots of zest and sparkle. She is an extrovert and one of life's gamblers, and even when things are bad she

Optimists tend to hold their fingers apart because they are so receptive to life.

This square on the fate line shows a setback from which the person will recover. Such resilience comes naturally to optimists.

believes that better times are just around the corner.

Now look at the fingertips. These are most likely to be spatulate, which is another sign of positive thinking and the ability to take risks. Spatulate fingertips also show the inventiveness that a born optimist needs when thinking her way round problems and finding clever solutions. In addition, she may have at least one tented arch on her fingertips to show enthusiasm.

Ask the person to hold her hands in a relaxed position. There will be gaps between the bases of her fingers, which show an open and friendly nature. There will also be a wide angle between her thumb and the side of her hand, indicating emotional generosity and the ability to accept whatever experiences life brings her.

JUPITER FINGER

Spend some time looking at this finger, because it is another indication of an optimistic nature. It should be long and well shaped to denote self-confidence and the ability to take the lead when necessary: Optimists are rarely completely passive. If this finger is very large, the person has an equally big ego and part of her optimism may come from a conviction that she deserves special treatment.

The Jupiter mount should also be well formed without being too big. If it has merged with the Saturn mount, it shows that the person is able to combine optimism with a sense of reality and thereby keeps her feet on the ground.

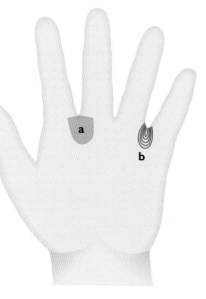

KEY POINTS
a *Mount between Jupiter and Saturn fingers*
b *Loop of humor*

An optimist is usually sociable and outgoing. You can expect to find evidence of her gregarious nature in her hands.

LOOP OF HUMOR

As you might imagine, an optimist does not take life too seriously. This does not mean she is irresponsible, but she is certainly able to bounce back from disappointments and setbacks. Therefore you are quite likely to find a loop of humor between her Apollo and Mercury fingers, and it will appear on both hands if she is a born optimist. When the loop is present, it shows that this person has a good sense of humor, a sunny nature and is extremely popular.

LINE OF APOLLO

Is someone an optimist because she is naturally lucky, or does her positive attitude attract positive experiences that might be described as luck? This is a moot point, but you may find some

of the answers by looking at the person's line of Apollo—the line of success, and traditionally also considered to be the line of good fortune. If it is strong and well formed, she will enjoy plenty of success in life and this will undoubtedly help to confirm her sense of optimism. She will be even luckier if, in addition to the line of Apollo, there is a star on her mount of Apollo, as this shows success and creative satisfaction.

THE PESSIMIST

As far as the pessimist is concerned, things can only ever get worse. He tends to concentrate on the gloomy and miserable side of life, convinced that the good times are outweighed by the bad and that optimists are nothing less than crazy.

There may be good reasons why someone is a pessimist, such as having weathered tremendous personal storms that did not work out well for him, and pessimists often make a joke of their rather negative attitude to life. However, someone who is deeply negative can eventually drive others away, which can make him lonely and even more pessimistic. He may also be depressed beneath his cynical laughter and in need of help.

Simple body language will give you clues about whether someone is a pessimist or an optimist.

THE SHAPE OF THE HAND

A true pessimist may have a water, air or earth hand, but is very unlikely to have a fire hand, because this is a sign of enthusiasm. Whatever its shape, the hand will feel limp and soft, as though all the life has gone out of it, especially if the person is depressed.

Look to see how he holds his hands when he is relaxed. If he keeps his fingers together, it shows that he is apprehensive and is unconsciously trying to hold on to what he has. If he also holds his thumbs close to his hands, for some reason he is afraid of being too open and generous.

THE FINGERS

What do the fingernails look like? If there are white flecks on them, the person has been feeling nervous for some time, as these flecks take several months to grow out of the nail.

You can also check to see whether he bites his nails because biting your

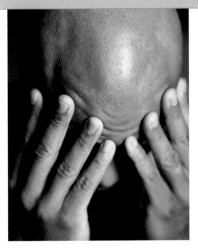

A pessimist has a tendency to make the worst of all his problems because he generally expects the worst.

nails is another classic sign of tension and nervousness.

Now look at the joints of the fingers, which will be knotted. These show that he spends a lot of time thinking things through and analyzing situations. He may therefore have a tendency to worry about the future and rehash unpleasant experiences from the past.

The Saturn finger will tell you a lot about the person's mental state. If it is much bigger or thicker than his other fingers, it shows that he has a tendency to make the worst of his problems and to feel oppressed by them. If he wears a ring on this finger rather than any other, he is unconsciously trying to boost his sense of security.

The mount of Saturn will also give you important information. If it is very large, it shows a tendency toward pessimism, especially if the person is regularly expected to take on more than his fair share of responsibility at the expense of more enjoyable pursuits. Another indication that he has learned to sacrifice his own needs for the sake of others, at some cost to himself, is if the Apollo finger leans toward the Saturn finger.

A grill on the mount of Saturn shows that he is going through a dispiriting and miserable time. However, the good news is that the grill will disappear when the problems ease.

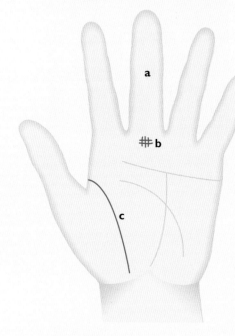

KEY POINTS
a *Thick Saturn finger*
b *Grill on the mount of Saturn*
c *Almost straight life line*

Here are other indications of a pessimistic nature. Note the heavy Saturn finger and the narrow gap beneath this finger between the heart and head lines.

HEAD LINE

The head line is another essential indicator of mental state. If it is weak and thin, it shows someone who is easily disappointed and finds it hard to think positively. If there are chains and islands on the head line, or short lines that cross it, he is prone to worry and uncertainty, and at times struggles to think rationally because he is so influenced by fearful thoughts.

Where does the head line end? If it swoops down to end on the mount of the Moon, he has an active imagination, but it may not always work in his favor because it can give him a tendency to fear the worst.

THE DIPLOMAT

How is it that some people always manage to be tactful while others have an unerring instinct for saying the wrong thing or being oblivious to the atmosphere around them?

What we are looking for here are signs of diplomacy in the hand. This is not only a valuable social skill, but a gift that someone can use in her career, perhaps by working in sales or personnel.

There are no outright signs of diplomacy in the hand, but there are many other indications that will tell you whether or not someone is tactful. If you look at your own hand you will see the level of your own ability to choose the right words, and some of your discoveries could come as a surprise.

A born diplomat takes the trouble to put others at ease immediately.

THE SHAPE OF THE HAND

When someone is diplomatic, she is able to communicate in a very sophisticated way, so you would expect her to have an air hand: the shape that corresponds to good communication skills and the ability to connect with other people on a mental level. In addition, someone with an air hand is not ruled by her emotions, so she is unlikely to have dramatic outbursts that upset everyone around her.

People with water hands also have the ability to be very tactful, thanks to their thoughtful, quiet and peaceful natures. They usually take great care not to upset others and find it easy to adapt to their surroundings.

This woman's fingers bend back slightly, showing flexibility and adaptability.

THE FINGERS

Now look at the person's fingers. Ideally they should be pointed or conic. If they are pointed, they show consideration and sensitivity toward others; if they are conic, they indicate an easy-going personality.

Can you see any composite whorls on the fingertips? These are an excellent indication of diplomacy, because they show that the person is able to see two sides to every story. This does not help her to reach important decisions, but it is invaluable when talking to other people or trying to mediate in an argument. Composite whorls are quite rare, so if you cannot find any, you should look for loops instead. If these form the majority of the fingerprint patterns on someone's hand, she is easy-going, good-natured and adaptable.

The fingernails also tell you about someone's diplomatic skills. If the nails are long and broad, she is patient, forbearing and broad-minded.

THE THUMB

How flexible is the thumb? You are looking for a thumb whose top joint bends back slightly without being completely double-jointed. Such flexibility reveals someone who adapts to her surroundings and therefore has a good measure of other people.

Another excellent indication of diplomacy is a waisted thumb, which shows tact and sensitivity.

RING OF SOLOMON

When someone is diplomatic, she has an instinctive understanding of how other people think and feel. This is

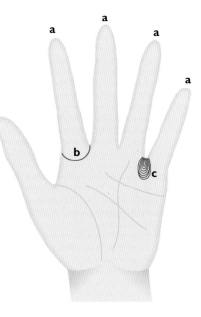

KEY POINTS
a *Pointed fingers*
b *Ring of Solomon*
c *Loop of humor*

often shown by the ring of Solomon, which curves around the mount of Jupiter. It is a classic indication of someone who is interested in psychology and may even study it, either professionally or in her spare time. Diplomacy is not only the ability to pacify others, but also involves being able to say difficult things in a tactful way, and a good knowledge of human nature is a valuable attribute.

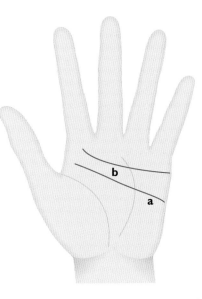

KEY POINTS
a *Long head line*
b *Space between head and heart lines*

Expert tip

Take a look at the space between the heart and head lines. It should be fairly wide, to show broad-mindedness. If someone is intolerant of another person's opinions, she is unlikely to be tactful when talking to them.

HEART LINE

Consideration for other people's feelings is reflected in the heart line. It should be gently curved, to indicate compassion, with many small lines running off it to show emotional connections with others.

THE TRAVELER

The world has shrunk during the past century as travel has become the preserve of everyone, and not just the rich or adventurous. More of us are traveling farther away each year, and new areas of the world are opening up to tourism. Yet not everyone wants to leave the comfort and security of the home for the uncertainties of unknown destinations. So what is it that makes someone a traveler, and can you see these indications in the palm?

Where to go next? An instinctive traveler often has a wish-list of destinations he is longing to visit.

THE SHAPE OF THE HAND

A committed traveler is most likely to have a fire or air hand. Someone with a fire hand will enjoy the stimulus, excitement and sense of adventure that comes from discovering new places, and will look on the journey as an important part of that experience. He is unlikely to want to return to the same destination year after year, because that strikes him as boring.

Someone with an air hand enjoys travel because of the chance it offers him to meet new people. He will make a point of learning at least a few words of the local language, if it differs from his own, because he gets so much pleasure from communicating with others.

Now look at the width of the person's palms. The wider these are, the more he craves wide open spaces and fresh air. In itself, this is not an indication of the urge to travel, but it does show that he is more likely to opt

The owner of a fire hand enjoys taking unusual and adventurous holidays.

for the countryside than a town or city when choosing a holiday destination.

THE FINGERS

What shape are the fingertips? If they are spatulate, the person gets a real buzz from travel and will enjoy experimenting with new or unusual

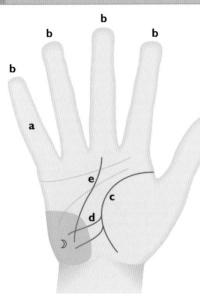

Take a look at the Mercury finger. If this is long and well formed, it shows a capacity for languages. Therefore this can be a sign of the traveler who enjoys speaking the local language, even if he can only string a few sentences together, and who always carries a phrase book around with him for the sheer pleasure of working out the meaning of signposts and menus.

MOUNT OF THE MOON

One of the meanings of this mount is travel, so you will want to examine it carefully. Can you see any horizontal lines running across this mount? If so, they indicate memorable or significant journeys that the person either has taken or will be taking. They run in chronological order from the base of the wrist upward toward the mount of Mercury. Look at both hands when examining this mount, because if you find these travel lines only on the

KEY POINTS

a *Long and well-formed Mercury finger*
b *Fingers with spatulate tips*
c *Very curved life line*
d *Strong lines branching off from life line toward the mount of the Moon*
e *Fate line starting on mount of the Moon*

destinations. If the fingertips are square, he will want his destination to be a home from home, and therefore as familiar as possible.

nondominant hand, it means that the person would love to travel, but something, such as lack of money or opportunity, is stopping him.

LIFE LINE

Does the life line have a good curve? If it swings out toward the center of the palm, it shows that the person is outgoing and interested in what life has to offer him.

Where does the life line end? If it finishes very close to the mount of the Moon, or actually on it, that person is a born traveler and may even emigrate to another country at some point in his life. This is also shown if several strong lines branch off from the life line and run across to the mount of the Moon.

Travel is also shown by small lines that start at the life line and point toward the mount of the Moon. These lines do not cross the life line, but start on the side of it closest to the mount of the Moon.

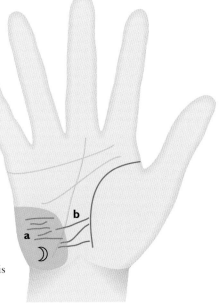

KEY POINTS

a *Travel lines on the mount of the Moon*
b *Lines running from near the life line toward the mount of the Moon*

THE MYSTIC

If you are reading this book it probably means that you have an interest in psychic matters and believe that we have six senses rather than five. Although not every palmist is psychic, most mystics have an intuitive sense that will develop as they continue to practice their art and this can happen to you, too.

The popular image of someone who is psychic is that she looks rather strange, that she is continually communing with her spirit guides and that the lights flicker whenever she walks into a room. More reliable and less stereotypical indications can come from examining someone's palm, although you will probably want to practice on your own hands first.

Someone who is mystical has an intense and rewarding inner life. She finds it sustaining and enriching.

THE FINGERS

These are more indicative of psychic ability than the shape of the hands. If someone has more pointed fingertips than any other type, she is intuitive

and able to tune into atmospheres. This tendency is increased if she has pointed Jupiter fingers, which are quite rare. If one or both of these fingers is pointed, she has a strong attraction to psychic and mystical topics, and may well show signs of psychic ability herself.

A long Apollo finger can be another sign of interest in spiritual and mystical matters, and this will be emphasized if the finger is pointed.

RING OF SOLOMON

Although this curved line on the mount of Jupiter is now considered to be a sign of psychological insight, it was traditionally believed to indicate psychic ability. It is often seen on the hands of astrologers, palmists and tarot readers, as well as on the hands of anyone else who makes conscious use of her intuition and instincts, and who needs to establish a strong psychological connection with other

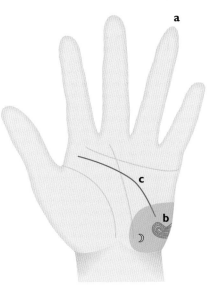

KEY POINTS
a *Long pointed Apollo finger*
b *Loop on the mount of the Moon*
c *Head line curving onto the mount of the Moon*

people. For instance, you may see the ring of Solomon on the hand of someone who instinctively knows the identity of a telephone caller before she picks up the phone.

MOUNT OF THE MOON

Look carefully to see whether there is a skin pattern, such as an arch or loop, on this mount, because that will show psychic talents. These skills will be emphasized if the patterns appear on both palms. It can be difficult to see such skin markings, especially on a hand with many subsidiary lines, unless you take a palm print and can pore over it.

LA CROIX MYSTIQUE

This cross sometimes appears in the space between the heart and head lines. As its name suggests, it is linked to intuition, an interest in mysticism and psychic talents. If it appears near the mount of Jupiter, it shows that the person has a tendency to use her psychic gifts to boost her ego, such as making a big fuss about being telepathic or having ESP. If the cross appears in the middle of the palm or partly consists of the fate

KEY POINTS

a La Croix Mystique *partially formed by fate line*

b *Long line of Apollo*

line, she will take her talents seriously and may make a living from them in some way.

LINE OF INTUITION

The line of intuition forms a semicircle around the outer edge of the palm and runs from the mount of the Moon to the mount of Mercury. It is rare, so you will not see it very often, but when you do it signifies great powers of intuition. It also describes spiritual values. Despite its name, it is a variation on the line of Mercury, which usually runs from the fate line up to the mount of Mercury.

LINE OF APOLLO

Traditionally associated with success and wealth, this line can also show a strong sense of spirituality and a need to express yourself. It should be strongly marked and long, which in itself is unusual because the line of Apollo is normally quite short.

A spiritual quality can take many forms, from belonging to an organized religion to worshipping nature.

THE LONER

Advertisers, magazines and television programs often give the impression that we should all spend our spare time being sociable and gregarious, and increasing our circle of friends. This suits some people very well, but it is the last thing others want. The fact is that we all have different social needs, and while some of us cannot survive without continual contact from friends and family, others are perfectly happy to enjoy their own company and mix only occasionally with the rest of the world.

You probably already know which category you fall into, or perhaps you are a combination of both. But what about some of the people in your life? Might a few of your discoveries come as a surprise? And what do you look for when you want to find out if someone is a loner?

When someone is a loner he instinctively holds his fingers and thumbs close together in an unconscious desire to keep the rest of the world at bay.

THE RELAXED HAND

Ask the person to hold his hands in a relaxed position, because this will give you major clues about his psychological type. Someone who enjoys his own company and prefers to be left alone has a closed hand when it is relaxed. As a result, he either holds his thumbs and fingers together (which effectively protects him from the rest of the world) or holds his fingers very close together (also a protective gesture, showing that he is self-contained).

If he holds his thumbs close to the sides of his hands, he is reticent and reluctant to give too much of himself away to anyone else. If the angle between his thumb and hand is smaller on his dominant hand, he has learned to protect himself after unpleasant experiences in the past. If the angle is smaller on the nondominant hand, he is instinctively shy and reserved, but is making heroic attempts to overcome these traits.

A Saturn finger that leans toward the Apollo finger shows someone who values having time to himself.

LONG FINGERS

If someone is a true loner, he will have long, knotty fingers in addition to some of the other characteristics described here. These show that he likes to live in his mind, and is introspective and analytical.

MERCURY FINGER

However, the rule about having long fingers may not apply to the Mercury finger, because this can be short on some people who prefer their own company. A short Mercury finger shows that it is difficult for someone to communicate with others, and he may also be emotionally immature. Emotional problems can also be suggested when the Mercury finger sits lower on the palm than the other fingers. This person may be very shy or insecure, or may worry about the way he communicates with others.

If he likes to keep a part of himself completely private, you will be able to see this because he will hold his Mercury finger away from the other fingers. He will do this quite instinctively, and you will be able to see it when he gestures with his hands. He may emphasize this sense of separation from everyone else by wearing a ring on one or both Mercury fingers. If so, take careful note of what the ring looks like, because this will give you farther clues about his state of mind.

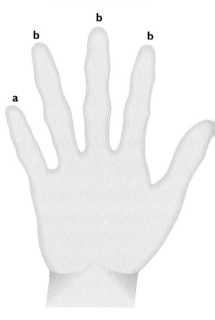

KEY POINTS
a *Short Mercury finger set low down on the hand and looking separate*
b *Long, knotty fingers*

SATURN FINGER

Saturn is the finger that rules responsibility and the tendency to take life seriously, so if someone is very reclusive you will be able to see it in his Saturn finger. If this finger is longer than normal, he has a serious attitude to life. It may also curve toward the Apollo finger, which shows a need for lots of time to himself and a tendency to put duty before pleasure.

An emphasis on the Saturn fingers and mounts indicates someone who takes his responsibilities very seriously.

MOUNT OF SATURN

When this mount is well developed, the person in question likes his own company and usually prefers it to being with other people whom he does not really care for or finds too frivolous and superficial.

THE CROSSPATCH

We have all met crosspatches—those people who seem to be permanently annoyed or angry. They manage to take offense at the most innocent remark and are apparently spoiling for a fight at any time of the day or night. Even if they ask a simple question, it is often phrased as a challenge. Unfortunately these irritable moods can be highly infectious, setting off everyone else, unless such people are able to keep an iron grip on their reactions and stay calm.

Here are some guidelines on what to look for if you suspect that someone is permanently irritable. These pointers are particularly useful if you are meeting a prospective boss or colleague, or trying to get the measure of a new neighbor, because even if the crosspatch is on her best behavior you will soon get a good idea of her true nature.

THE SHAPE OF THE HAND

If someone has a tendency to fly into a rage, she is most likely to have a fire hand. This shows that she is impulsive, assertive and spontaneous, although of course many people with

When the thumb is held outside a clenched fist it indicates aggression.

fire hands manage to control their tempers perfectly well, so the shape of the hand is not in itself conclusive proof that someone is always irritable.

THE THUMB

A very important indication of someone's character is the thumb, so you should pay close attention to it. If it is very heavy and thick, it belongs to someone with a domineering personality who likes to get her own way. Watch out if, when viewed from the side, the top phalange of the thumb is very bulbous and thick because that shows obstinacy and aggression. You may want to put as much distance as possible between yourself and this person, especially if the thumb is short and low-set on her hand, as this means that she has a violent, ungovernable temper and may also lack intelligence.

How flexible is the thumb? A stiff thumb shows someone who is reliable,

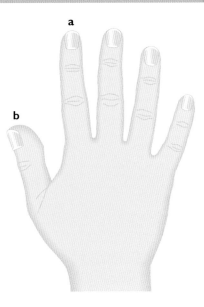

KEY POINTS
a *Long Jupiter finger*
b *Short, low-set thumb with bulbous tip*

but also likely to be very stubborn, which means that she will be reluctant to back down in arguments. If the thumb is so flexible that it forms an exaggerated curve, she is adaptable to the point of being able to say whatever anyone else wants to hear.

KEY POINTS
a *Short Mercury finger*
b *Short wide nails*

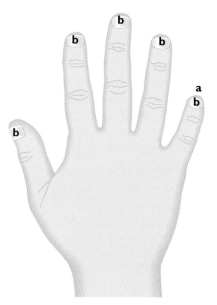

JUPITER FINGER

A normal Jupiter finger shows a healthy ego, but if the finger is very long that person will be extremely proud and sure of herself. By itself this does not make her irritable and angry, but if it is combined with several other indications of a bad temper, it can mean she is arrogant and always has to have the last word.

THE NAILS

These are an important indication of someone's temper, and it should be easy to observe someone's nails during the course of a normal conversation. Provided that the person is not wearing nail polish or false nails, you can read her temper from the color of her nails. If her nails are naturally red, she has an equally fiery temper.

Short nails belong to someone who is impatient and finds fault with others. If the nails are wide as well as short, she is extremely critical and tends to blame other people for her own problems. All these tendencies will be increased if there is a gap between the fingernail and the top of the finger.

Crosspatches find it difficult to control their reactions to stressful situations.

Expert tip

If the Mercury finger is very short, the person lacks maturity and may also struggle with emotional difficulties. She may express these through childish tantrums or a determination to get her own way.

GLOSSARY

Air hand One of the four hand shapes, consisting of a square palm and longer fingers, and indicating good communication skills.

Angle of rhythm The point where the base of the thumb meets the wrist.

Angle of timing The joint at the bottom of the thumb's middle phalange.

Apollo finger The third or ring finger, signifying success and artistic ability.

Arch A skin pattern showing efficiency and practicality.

Body language The science of analyzing behavior through gestures and other physical movements.

Bracelets of Neptune The group of lines at the base of the wrist, signifying health.

Break An interruption in the energy of a line.

Chain A series of small islands that appear on a line.

Chirognomy The study of the shape of the hand.

Chiromancy The study of the lines on the palm.

Composite whorl A rare skin pattern showing the ability to see two sides to every story.

Conic The description given to the rounded tip of a finger or thumb.

Cross A mark created by two lines crossing, which is associated with difficulties.

Dermatoglyphics The study of fingerprints and skin ridges.

Dominant hand The hand with which a person writes.

Droplet The small pad of flesh on the top phalange of the fingers that signifies sensitivity.

Earth hand One of the four hand shapes, consisting of a square palm and short fingers, and indicating a practical nature.

Family ring The line on the palm that marks the point where the middle phalange of the thumb joins the palm, showing family feeling.

Fate line The line that runs from the base of the palm to the base of the fingers, showing someone's path through life.

Fire hand One of the four hand shapes, consisting of a long palm and short fingers, and indicating enthusiasm.

Girdle of Venus The line that can appear above the heart line at the top of the palm, showing emotional sensitivity.

Grille Small horizontal and vertical lines that signify temporary problems.

Head line The lower line that runs across the middle of the palm, signifying the way someone thinks.

Heart line The upper line that runs across the middle of the palm, signifying the ability to feel and express emotions.

Influence lines Tiny lines that run off a major or minor line, showing that it has been influenced in some way.

Inner mount of Mars The fleshy pad below the mount of Jupiter and above the mount of Venus, signifying physical courage.

Island A small circle that appears on a line, showing a lack of focus.

Jupiter finger The first or index finger, signifying leadership qualities and confidence.

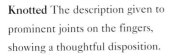

Knotted The description given to prominent joints on the fingers, showing a thoughtful disposition.

La Croix Mystique A cross that appears in the space between the head and heart lines, showing an interest in the occult and spiritual matters.

Life line The line that curves around the base of the thumb, describing someone's health and general vitality.

Line of Apollo The small line that appears under the Apollo finger, signifying success and wealth.

Line of children A short vertical line rising from the line of marriage.

Line of interference A small line that crosses a major or minor line and blocks its energy.

Line of intuition A variation on the line of Mercury, forming a semicircle from the mount of the Moon up to the mount of Mercury, and showing intuition.

Line of marriage A small line found on the side of the palm between the heart line and the base of the Mercury finger, showing an important relationship.

Line of Mars The curved line that runs down the mount of Venus, showing physical strength.

Line of Mercury The line that runs up the palm to the mount of Mercury, signifying health.

Lines of influence *see* Influence lines.

Loop A skin pattern showing flexibility and the ability to get on well with others.

Loop of humor A loop skin pattern between the Apollo and Mercury fingers, signifying an optimistic attitude to life.

Loop of seriousness A loop skin pattern between the Jupiter and Saturn fingers, showing a serious attitude to life.

Medical stigmata A collection of short lines under the Mercury finger, showing the urge to help others.

Mercury finger The fourth or little finger, signifying communication skills.

Mount A pad of flesh found in a particular place on the palm.

Mount of Apollo The fleshy pad beneath the Apollo finger, signifying artistic ability and a sociable nature.

Mount of Jupiter The fleshy pad beneath the Jupiter finger, signifying ambition and ego.

Mount of Mars *see* Inner mount of Mars; outer mount of Mars.

Mount of Mercury The fleshy pad beneath the Mercury finger, signifying communication and business ability.

Mount of the Moon The fleshy pad at the base of the palm opposite the thumb, signifying imagination and travel.

Mount of Saturn The fleshy pad beneath the Saturn finger, signifying self-control and responsibility.

Mount of Venus The fleshy pad covering the base of the thumb, signifying vitality and the ability to show affection.

Nondominant hand A person's non-writing hand.

Outer mount of Mars The fleshy pad below the mount of Mercury and above the mount of the Moon, signifying moral courage.

Pad *see* Droplet.

Percussion The shape of the outer edge of the palm; when curved, it indicates creativity.

Phalange A section of a finger or thumb.

Plain of Mars The area in the center of the palm, signifying confidence.

Pointed The description given to the pointed tip of a finger or thumb.

Ring of Solomon The curved line that encircles the mount of Jupiter, signifying a good understanding of human nature.

Saturn finger The middle or second finger, indicating responsibility and authority.

Simian line A single line that combines the head and heart lines.

Sister line A line that runs parallel to a major or minor line, thereby giving it support.

Smooth The shape of a finger where the joints are hardly visible, signifying impulsiveness.

Spatulate The description given to the tip of a finger or thumb when it widens slightly at the top.

Square The description given to the tip of a finger or thumb when it is roughly square; also the name given to small lines arranged in a square formation around a break in a line.

Star A star-shaped mark on the hand that indicates difficulties.

Teacher's square A small square found on the mount of Jupiter that is

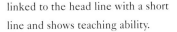

linked to the head line with a short line and shows teaching ability.

Tented arch A rare skin pattern showing enthusiasm.

Three worlds The three horizontal divisions of the palm, ruling the mind and spirit, practical matters, and the material world.

Triangle A triangular shape made up of lines on the palm, showing knowledge and technical ability.

Waisted The pinched shape of a phalange, and especially the middle phalange of the thumb.

Water hand One of the four hand shapes, consisting of a long palm and long fingers, and indicating sensitivity.

Whorl A skin pattern showing individuality.

INDEX

ACKNOWLEDGMENTS

Many people have helped to make this book what it is. I would like to thank everyone at Godsfield Press who worked on the book, but especially Brenda Rosen for her enthusiasm and her meticulous attention to detail, and Clare Churly for all her help. Many thanks, too, to my agent, Chelsey Fox, and my husband, Bill Martin, for all their understanding and support.

PICTURE ACKNOWLEDGMENTS

Corbis UK Ltd 253, 286, 288, 336, 342; /Peter Beck 351; /Bettmann 19; /Ed Bock 17; /Horace Bristol 15; /Cameron 267; /Jim Craigmyle 324; /ER Productions 21; /Randy Faris 298; /Jon Feingersh 6, 35, 328; /Patrik Giardino 33; /Gary Houlder 325; /Stuart Hughes 367; /Michael Keller 346; /Helen King 31; /Jutta Klee 265; /Simon Marcus 272; /Steve McDonough 348; /Tim McGuire 304; /Roy McMahon 255; /Gabe Palmer 20; /Jose Luis Pelaez Inc. 291, 362, 363; /Steve Prezant 350; /Anthony Redpath 316; /Pete Saloutos 16; /Ariel Skelley 318; /Tom Stewart 295; /LWA-Dann Tardif 257, 329; /LWA-Stephen Welstead 374; /Alison Wright 322. **Creatas** 274. **Digital Vision** 340, 378, 381. **Image Source** 36, 258, 281, 284, 294, 306, 373, 377. **Mary Evans Picture Library** 9, 11. **Getty Images** 354, 359/David C. Ellis 357; /Chris Fortuna 282; /Julia Fullerton-Batten 38 left; /Don Klumpp 300; /Photomondo 13; /Justin Pumfrey 37; /Michel Setboun 18; /Paul Thomas 343. **Octopus Publishing Group Limited** 34, 38 right, 57, 276; /Richard Francis 332; /Mike Hemsley at Walter Gardiner Photography 22 right, 55, 312; /Alistair Hughes 278; /Mark Newcombe 334; /Peter Pugh-Cook 40 top left, 67; /William Reavell 12; /Russell Sadur 22 left, 260; /Ian Wallace 5, 56. **Photolibrary.com** 32; /Nancy R. Cohen 50; /Dech 320; /Gategno 370; /Andreas Koerner 302; /Image Source 269; /Stock Montage 10; /Robert Whitman 54. **Photodisc** 1, 2, 3, 40 bottom right, 42, 44, 45, 46, 48, 64, 66, 98, 138, 250, 262, 268, 309, 310, 313, 338, 358, 366. **TopFoto**/Charles Walker 8.

Executive Editor Brenda Rosen
Managing Editor Clare Churly
Executive Art Editor Sally Bond
Designer Annika Skoog and Pia Ingham for
    Cobalt Id
Illustrator Kuo Kang Chen
Picture Researcher Sally Claxton and
    Jennifer Veall
Production Manager Louise Hall